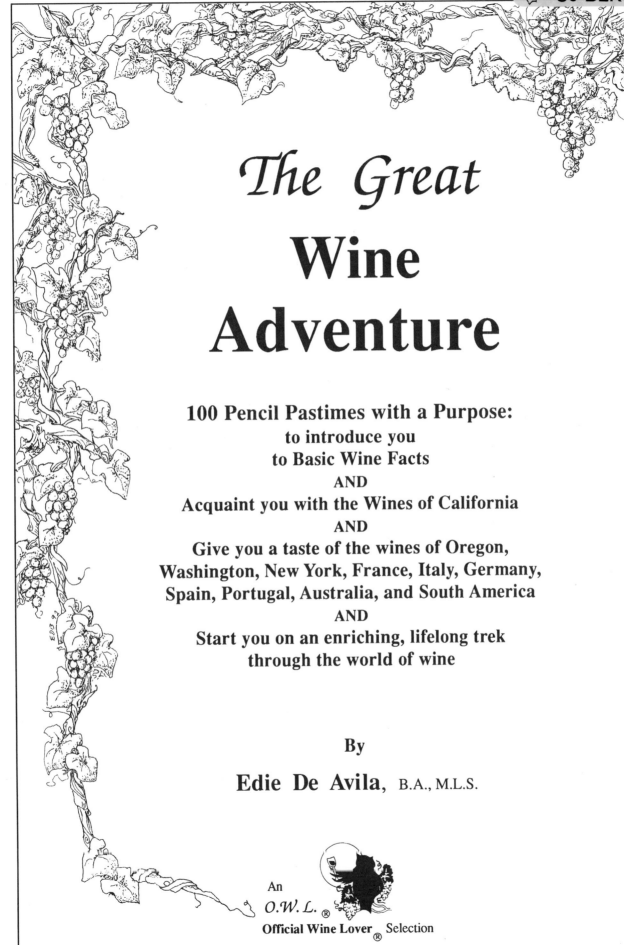

The Great
Wine
Adventure

100 Pencil Pastimes with a Purpose:
to introduce you
to Basic Wine Facts
AND
Acquaint you with the Wines of California
AND
Give you a taste of the wines of Oregon,
Washington, New York, France, Italy, Germany,
Spain, Portugal, Australia, and South America
AND
Start you on an enriching, lifelong trek
through the world of wine

By

Edie De Avila, B.A., M.L.S.

An
O.W.L. ®
Official Wine Lover ® Selection

Published by...

Port Royal

Publications & Designs, U.S.A.

16228 Estella Avenue
Cerritos CA U.S.A. 90701-1510
(310) 865-2888

Additional editing by Mary Ann Failla
Book cover by Edie De Avila and Mary Ann Failla

The Great Wine Adventure
Contents

O.W.L.®

Hello!

An owl appreciating wine? Why not? After all, owls are wise, and they contribute to good wine by keeping unwanted birds and rodents out of the vineyards. (We don't chase away as many birds and rodents as the grape growers would like – why should we kill off our food supply? But we help a little).

My name is **O.W.L.®**, which stands for **Official Wine Lover,®** and it's my pleasure to introduce you to *The Great Wine Adventure–* the completely revised and updated version of *The Great Wine Puzzle Book*. These pencil games have a purpose – they make it easy for you to understand wine.

You don't need to know a thing about wine to complete our puzzles. As you solve them, you'll uncover the story of wine's grapes, production, tastes, smells, colors, chemistry, labels, glasses, bottles, people, regions, traditions, and trends.

We divided this book into 3 sections for you:

I. **Wine Basics** ....Fundamental wine facts, starting on page 7.
II. **Travel Section** ....First-class tours of wine regions and methods in California, with side excursions to the U.S., France, Italy, Germany, Spain, Portugal, Australia, and South America. They start on page 49.
III. **Wine Fanfare** ....Our knapsack of wine mysteries starts on page 104. You can solve these by using the facts that you learned in Sections I and II.

Remember, you can solve all of the puzzles without knowing anything about wine and without using any other books.

If you're new to wine, start with the **Wine Basics** section and play our pencil games pretty much in order to the end of the book. If you fancy yourself the very devil with wine knowledge, jump in anywhere you like.

In the back of the book you'll find all of the **Answers** to our brainteasers (page 114), a **Pronouncing Guide** (page 124), and an **Interesting Reading List** (page 126).

And now, friend, begin...

WINE...

...it transformeth a man into a beast,
decayeth health, poisoneth the breath,
destroyeth natural heat,...deformeth the
face, rotteth the teeth,...and maketh
a man contemptible...

Sir Walter Raleigh

This from a man who introduced *smoking* to the entire known world?

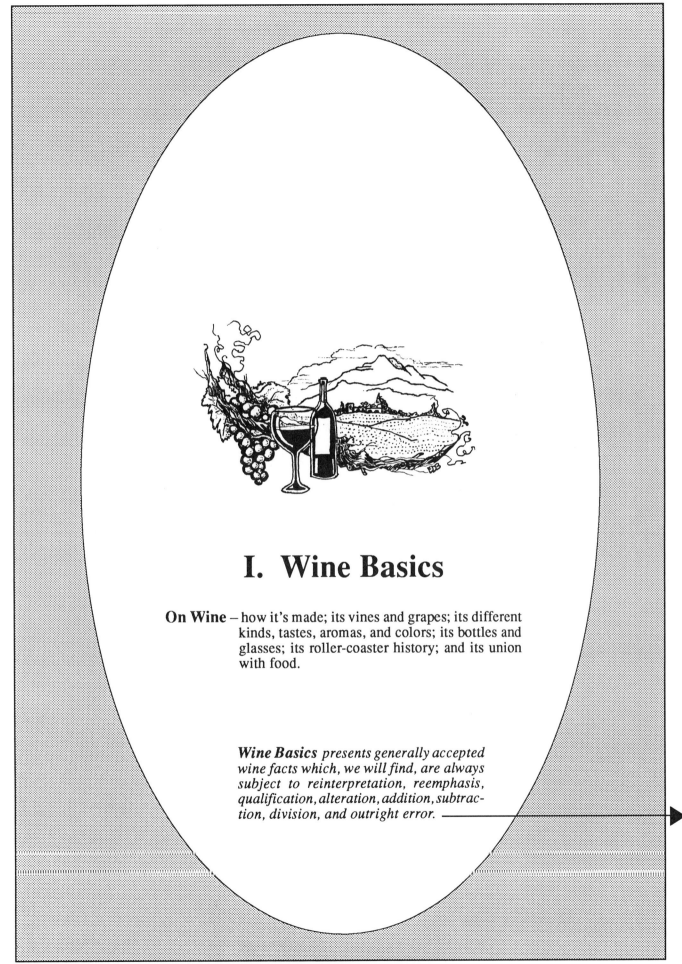

I. Wine Basics

On Wine – how it's made; its vines and grapes; its different kinds, tastes, aromas, and colors; its bottles and glasses; its roller-coaster history; and its union with food.

Wine Basics presents generally accepted wine facts which, we will find, are always subject to reinterpretation, reemphasis, qualification, alteration, addition, subtraction, division, and outright error.

1. Why Wine?

Why are you interested in wine? We wrote a few of our own reasons below. Out of all the words we used, 28 of them hid themselves in our wordfind: look up, down, forwards, backwards, and diagonally to find them.

Some reasons to like wine:

1. **The flavor and aroma** ... Wine is a delicious food. It stimulates taste and scent sensations and enhances the flavors of other foods.

2. **The variety** .... Such choices! Thousands of reds, whites, rosés, and sparklers – all of them influenced by different grapes, places, and methods; all of them appealing to our changing moods.

3. **The challenge** .... Winemaking has an ancient history, rich traditions, and fascinating technology: we can never learn it all.

4. **The people** .... Where wine is appreciated, all classes and types come together. Whether they are growers, makers, sellers, or enjoyers, wine people make unusually interesting company.

Now, uncover 28 of these words in our wordfind. ⟶ ⟶

WINE PEOPLE ARE SENSITIVE.

DAFFY DEFINITION: FLAVOR – a good turn done for someone; well-bred wines always do us a flavor.

Word List

FOOD	VARIETY
REDS	CHANGING
WINE	ENHANCES
AROMA	ENJOYERS
MOODS	TOGETHER
ROSÉS	APPEALING
FLAVOR	CHALLENGE
MAKERS	DELICIOUS
PEOPLE	SPARKLERS
WHITES	SENSATIONS
CHOICES	STIMULATES
GROWERS	TECHNOLOGY
HISTORY	TRADITIONS
SELLERS	INTERESTING

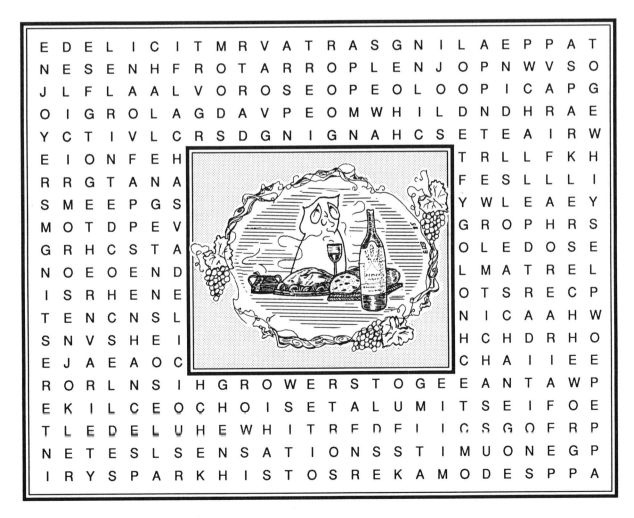

Three Main Styles Of Wine

Discover 3 basic styles, or types, of wine. Puzzles #2, #3, and #4 on these pages all have <u>underlined</u> words and blank spaces. Place the <u>underlined</u> words correctly onto the blanks. Then, read the boxed letters **DOWN** to reveal our 3 answers. One, two, three – GO!

2. Added Spirits

These wines have <u>spirits</u>, such as brandy (and <u>often</u> a <u>sweetener</u> <u>or</u> a <u>color</u>) added <u>before</u> <u>bottling</u>. They are <u>high</u> in alcohol – 18% to 20% – and can be sweet or <u>dry</u> (the opposite of sweet). Examples are ports, sherries, and Madeira wines.

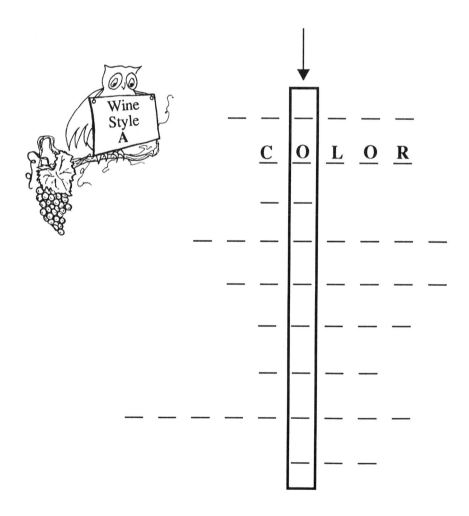

C O L O R

DAFFY DEFINITION: Champagne – an ache experienced by a prize-winning athlete.

3. With Food

These **fermented** wines can **be** red, white, or rosé, and they are usually designed **to accompany meals**. They contain up to 13 or 14% **alcohol**.

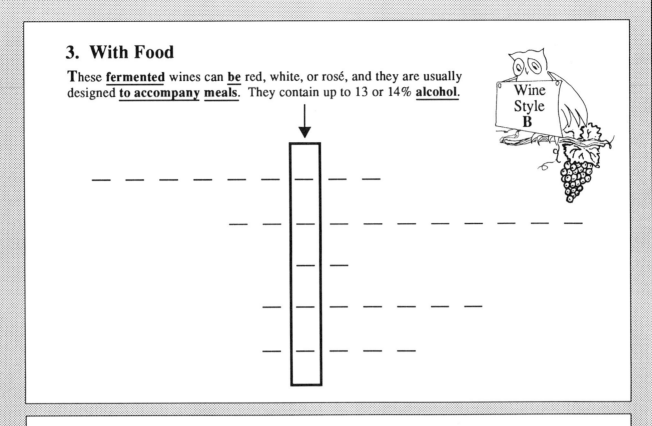

4. Let's Celebrate!

These wines, by one method or another, have CO_2 **bubbles speeding** through them. The **most** well-**known** of these are **France's Champagne** and **Italy's Asti spumante**. This kind of wine can be made **dry** to very sweet.

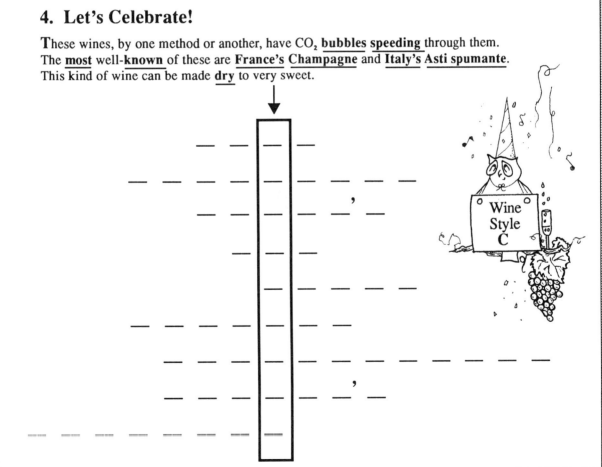

These 3 kinds of wine are also used in 2 special ways. Find out what they are on the next page.

Before And After

Hidden below are 2 traditional ways we use wine: find out what they are by playing Puzzles #5 and #6. *(Directions to play are with Puzzle #2 on pg. 10).*

5. Before

Some wines serve as "appetizer" wines. Dry, **chilled** **Champagne** or other dry whites, as well as dry, fortified Madeira or sherry, and very **light, fruity red** wines can delicately **anticipate** food. When a wine is served to **whet** the **appetite**, it's called an...

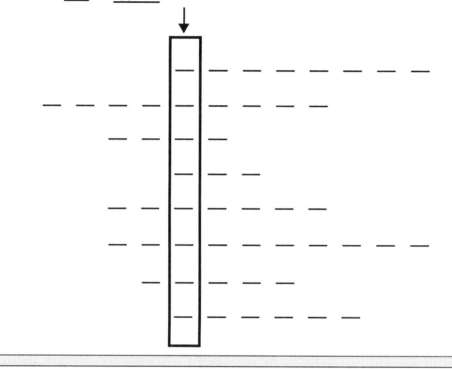

6. After

Some wines are served as **after-dinner**, sweetly **satisfying** treats. Some delicious examples are: sweet **Asti** spumante, golden **Sauternes**, rich **port**, **cream** sherry, and sweet Madeira and **Muscat** wines. Enjoyed at a meal's end, these wines are called _____ wines.

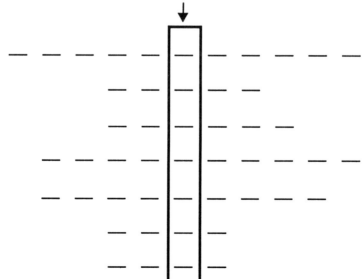

7. Varietal Vs. Blend

Explore the meaning of our title above. Here's how to do it: 5 adjoining letters in Barrel #1 connect to form a word (**blend**). We've placed **blend** on Blank #1 below. Now it's your turn – release the secret word trapped in Barrel #2, place it on Blank #2, and so on with the rest of the barrels. (Large barrels or casks, such as those used for sherry, are also called *butts*.)

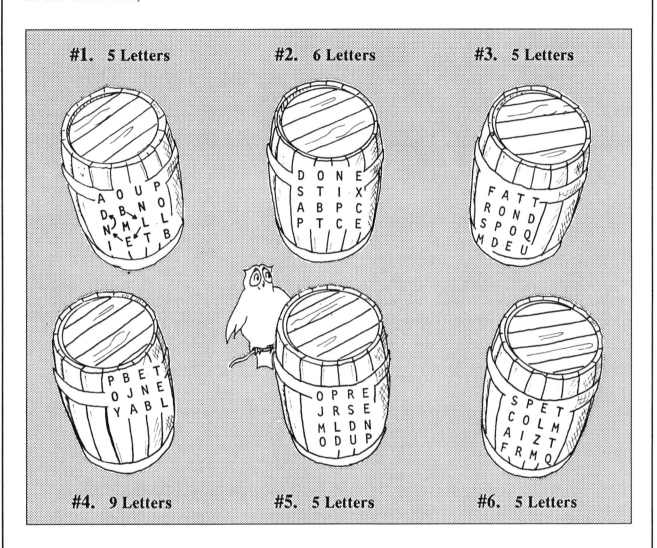

#1. 5 Letters **#2.** 6 Letters **#3.** 5 Letters

#4. 9 Letters **#5.** 5 Letters **#6.** 5 Letters

When you #5_____ #6_____ mignon, you plan to savor one particular food and you #2_____ it to be brought to its own unique perfection. A varietal wine is like that: one grape variety, such as Chardonnay, predominates even if small amounts of other grape varieties are added.

When you create a stew, you #1__**BLEND**__ different #3_____ , and marry them together into an #4_____ whole. Such are blended (also called generic) wines: they're constructed from several grape varieties.

Both varietal and blended wines can come from noble or lesser grapes and both can be delightful or disappointing.

8. Varietal Wines

A premium varietal wine is made mainly from one fine grape variety. The U.S. and some other countries name their varietal wines after the main grape in them (*California Cabernet Sauvignon* and *New York State Chardonnay*, for example).[1] Discover more varietal veracities! Answer the **Definitions**, then transfer the letters by number to the spaces below.

Definitions

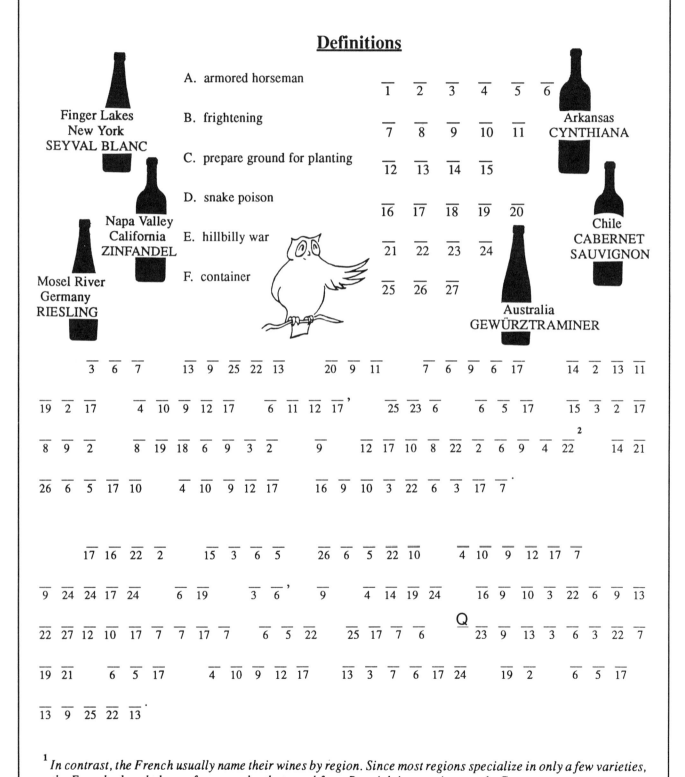

A. armored horseman

$\overline{1}$ $\overline{2}$ $\overline{3}$ $\overline{4}$ $\overline{5}$ $\overline{6}$

B. frightening

$\overline{7}$ $\overline{8}$ $\overline{9}$ $\overline{10}$ $\overline{11}$

C. prepare ground for planting

$\overline{12}$ $\overline{13}$ $\overline{14}$ $\overline{15}$

D. snake poison

$\overline{16}$ $\overline{17}$ $\overline{18}$ $\overline{19}$ $\overline{20}$

E. hillbilly war

$\overline{21}$ $\overline{22}$ $\overline{23}$ $\overline{24}$

F. container

$\overline{25}$ $\overline{26}$ $\overline{27}$

Finger Lakes
New York
SEYVAL BLANC

Napa Valley
California
ZINFANDEL

Mosel River
Germany
RIESLING

Arkansas
CYNTHIANA

Chile
CABERNET
SAUVIGNON

Australia
GEWÜRZTRAMINER

___
[1] *In contrast, the French usually name their wines by region. Since most regions specialize in only a few varieties, the French already know, for example, that a red from Beaujolais contains mostly Gamay grapes.*

[2] *In California, 25% of other varieties.*

9. Blended Wines

Put more than one grape variety into a wine? At one time in the U.S. most wines made from 2 or more grape varieties were called "generic" and were not considered premium. Not any more. Read our sentences below for the blending story. The **19 bold-lettered, <u>underlined</u>** words in our sentences are hiding out in this wordfind. Look up, down, across, backwards, and diagonally, and catch those little critters.

Washington State
RED WINE

California
CHIANTI

Australia
Vintage
PORT

Oregon State
MOUNTAIN
CLARET

California
BURGUNDY

Australia
SHERRY

Ohio State
CHABLIS

New York
State
CHAMPAGNE

Michigan
WHITE TABLE WINE

C	T	Y	S	A	G	D	E	M	A	N	D	I	N	G	C	M
H	N	R	T	M	E	P	A	M	T	R	A	R	D	B	O	E
I	A	R	A	E	N	T	O	A	A	B	E	C	O	U	U	T
C	I	E	L	D	E	C	R	R	E	S	G	E	N	R	N	H
H	H	H	E	A	I	T	I	E	T	Y	P	Z	O	G	T	O
A	C	S	A	R	M	T	E	R	C	H	A	P	M	U	R	D
M	E	Y	E	C	N	C	I	L	W	M	E	T	S	N	E	S
P	R	N	M	A	L	C	N	O	I	A	H	Y	T	D	S	P
A	E	A	I	A	T	R	Y	Y	N	A	S	G	N	Y	E	N
G	S	H	T	G	O	T	P	T	E	A	N	E	L	B	P	R
N	C	E	E	P	I	O	H	S	D	B	L	E	N	L	C	S
E	L	D	C	L	A	R	E	T	A	B	A	L	C	I	T	M
Y	E	N	A	C	Y	C	O	U	N	T	R	I	E	S	W	R
A	M	U	A	M	E	T	H	O	D	C	R	E	N	E	G	I
S	R	O	L	O	C	R	S	I	L	B	A	H	C	C	S	F

Europeans enjoy a long history of creating premium wines by mixing together different grape varieties. Early U.S. and Australian vintners blended too, and named their generic wines by <u>color</u> or after famous European wines and wine regions.* Some examples: <u>claret</u>, **<u>Chablis</u>**, **<u>Burgundy</u>**, <u>sherry</u>, <u>port</u>, **<u>Champagne</u>**, and **<u>Chianti</u>**. These wines, while often tasty, weren't at all the <u>same</u> as their **<u>European</u>** namesakes and they frequently used lower-quality grapes and <u>methods</u>. New World blends got little or no respect until <u>lately</u>.

Now, quality **<u>firms</u>** are raising **<u>generic</u>** winecrafting to an art. They blend several fine varieties into complex wines. Examples are: Cabernet Sauvignon + Merlot + Cabernet Franc reds and Sauvignon Blanc + Sémillon whites (both inspired by Bordeaux) and Rhône-style reds **<u>blended</u>** from varying combinations of Grenache, Syrah, and/or Mourvèdre.

*Europe's wine nations have been **<u>demanding</u>** that other **<u>countries</u> <u>restrict</u>** their use of **<u>traditional</u>** European wine names.

10. A Yeast Feast

Chemistry! Investigate the delicious changes it brings in winemaking. See the **Words** and the grid below? Just correctly place those words into the grid to give each word a number. Then, by number, fill the words onto the blanks on the facing page. We've done #25 to start you off.

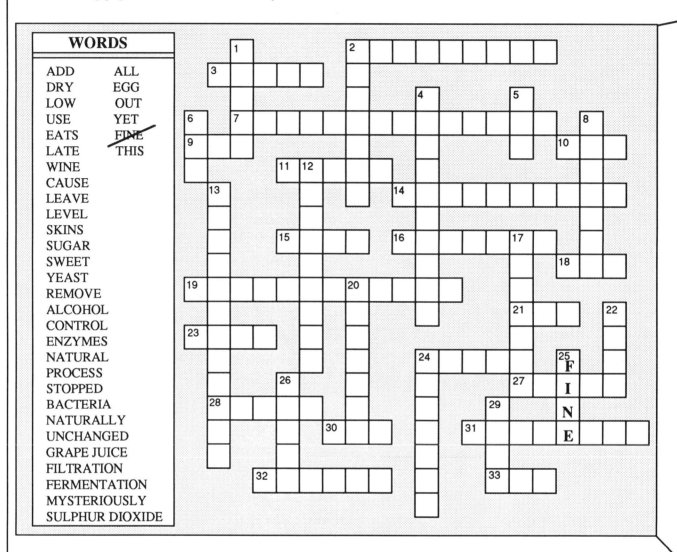

WORDS

ADD	ALL
DRY	EGG
LOW	OUT
USE	YET
EATS	~~FINE~~
LATE	THIS
WINE	
CAUSE	
LEAVE	
LEVEL	
SKINS	
SUGAR	
SWEET	
YEAST	
REMOVE	
ALCOHOL	
CONTROL	
ENZYMES	
NATURAL	
PROCESS	
STOPPED	
BACTERIA	
NATURALLY	
UNCHANGED	
GRAPE JUICE	
FILTRATION	
FERMENTATION	
MYSTERIOUSLY	
SULPHUR DIOXIDE	

Scientific Illustration #1: Fermentation (Actually, this isn't our first scientific illustration – it's our **only** scientific illustration.)

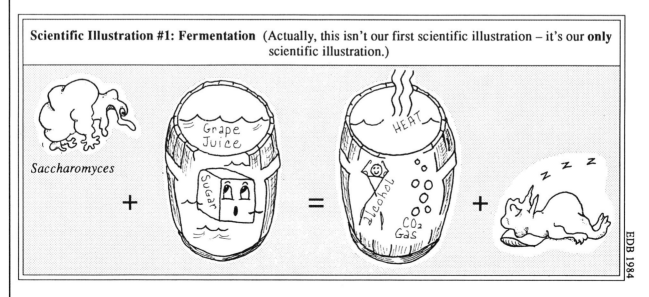

EDB 1984

• Grape juice contains (2D*_____ (11_____ . Somehow, local yeasts (13_____ appear on grape (27_____ and pounce on this (11_____ , turning it into (20_____ , carbon dioxide, and heat. This (8_____ is called (19_____ , and it's the (24A*_____ of wine.

• The more (11_____ that a (1_____ enzyme "(22_____," the more (20_____ it forms. When the (20_____ (3_____ reaches about 15%, the yeasts go dormant, then they're cleared from the (23_____ .

•(15_____ normally leaves the wine "(10_____," (meaning that it contains little or no (11_____). Sometimes, however, the (14_____ is so (28_____ that the (1_____ (17_____ make 15% (20_____ , doze off, and (26_____ much of the (11_____ (12_____ . This creates high- (20_____ , (21_____ (2A_____ (28_____ wines, often called "(29_____ harvest."

• If the harvested grapes are (6_____ in (2D_____ (11_____ , yeasts can be (16_____ before they "eat" it (30_____ . To make yeast particles sleep, vintners dose the wine with (7_____ , or they (18_____ refrigeration. They then clear all the yeast (9_____ of the wine by (25 FINE (4_____ . They can also (5_____ sediment collectors such as (33_____ whites or clay. If the (1_____ cells aren't removed, they will attract (31_____ and spoil the (23_____ .

• Modern winemakers usually (32_____ the (2D_____ (1_____ after quieting it with sulphur dioxide. They substitute predictable, pure (1_____ strains so that they can (24D_____ the (23_____'s complete progress. However, to use less SO_2 and to draw out unusual tastes and textures, more and more vintners (18_____ their grapes' (2A_____ – occurring yeasts.

*2D means 2 Down and 24A means 24 Across

DAFFY DEFINITION: Yeast – the opposite direction of ywest.

11. Making It – Red Wine

Pipes, pipes, and more pipes transport high-tech wine from one process to another. Follow our pipe system and journey through each red winemaking step, in order, only once. As you reach each numbered step, check the same number in our **Tour Directions** and see how your red wines are coming along.[1]

Tour Directions

1. **Crush** or press red (also called "black") grapes. Use a single red grape variety, or plan to blend several red varieties together.

2. **Move the fresh grape juice** (must) into fermentation vats. You can remove or include some or all of the skins, seeds, and stalks. The skins color the must[2] and the stalks and skins provide body, bitterness (that must be controlled), and tannin, the mouth-puckering compound that helps red wines to age well.

3. **Add yeast.** You can use the natural yeast on grape skins or introduce a special yeast culture. Fermentation begins. A cap of skins and stems floats on top of the warm fermenting must. Many winemakers pump the juice over itself and over this cap to draw out more color and tannin.

4. **As the wine ferments,** it throws off dead yeast cells and other residue. Pump the wine off these "lees" several times: they can damage the wine's taste. This is called "racking." Transfer the wine into a clean vat (oak, steel, or redwood).

5. **"Fine" the wine.** Remove sediment that escaped racking. Add a substance that settles to the bottom of the vat or barrel, carrying with it any suspended sediment. Choose from egg white, milk protein, gelatin, bentonite clay, or chemicals. Many modern winemakers also centrifuge the wine or pass it through sterilized porous filters and membranes. But some think that such modern methods take the "heart" out of the wine.[3]

6. **If you choose,** barrel the wine. The type of wood and microorganisms present in the barrels will add additional flavor and finish to the wine.

7. **Form the final wine you need.** You can make your reds into strong wines, able to age for 10 to 80 years. You can decide instead to form lighter, ready-to-drink table wines, or create festive sparkling wines or sweetened "pop" coolers.

[1] *Winemaking is faceted with exciting variations – carbonic maceration, malolactic and barrel fermentations, exotic yeast cultures. They're intriguing to investigate, so read about them soon in other books. (See our Interesting Reading section, p. 126.)*

[2] *Wines destined to become light red rosés are left on the black skins just a teensy; a smidge is also acceptable. (Really, just a few hours to a few days.)*

[3] *Also, a growing number of vintners proudly make completely unfiltered wines.*

12. Making It – White Wine

Temperature-controlled stainless steel tanks and oak barrels form the heart of modern white winemaking facilities. Travel our maze in numerical order. Stop at each white winemaking step only once. As you reach each numbered step, check the same number in our **Tour Directions** and see how your white wines are progressing.

> ## Tour Directions

1. **Press The Grapes.** Most white wines come from white grapes, but they can be made from red (also called "black") ones. An example is "white" Zinfandel. Grape juice is quickly removed from the black skins before they color it.

2. **Adjust Sugar.** Some white grapes don't contain enough sugar to insure proper fermentation, alcohol content, and acid balance. Winemakers then "chaptalize," or sweeten, the grape juice (*must*). They should do this under strict controls, and use grape, not cane, sugar. Californians, who cannot legally chaptalize, accuse New York, France, and Germany of overusing this process.

3. **Adjust Yeast.** Ferment the wine. In hot zones, use refrigeration and also a CO_2 or a nitrogen covering to keep out harmful heat and bacteria.

4. **You Can Stop Fermentation** part-way for a sweeter wine, or you can bottle your wine before fermentation is complete (to make some sparkling wines), or you can let the wine ferment until it is dry (unsweet).

5. **"Rack."** When you rack the wine, you clarify it by separating it from the "lees" (fermentation residue). Clear the wine more completely by centrifuging or fine-filtering it.

6. **Determine The Final Wine Type.** You might decide to bottle your wine for a quick consumption and profit, or choose to age and flavor it a bit in a barrel. Most white wines lack heavy acid, tannin, or other strong ingredients. This keeps them from aging and flowering in the bottle as long as many reds do.*

 * *However, some high-acid whites last well, and some high-sugar whites, such as French Sauternes, age beautifully for years in the bottle. High quality German whites also improve in the bottle for 3 to 10 years or more.*

DAFFY DEFINITION: Rack – torture the wine to make it confess and "come clean."

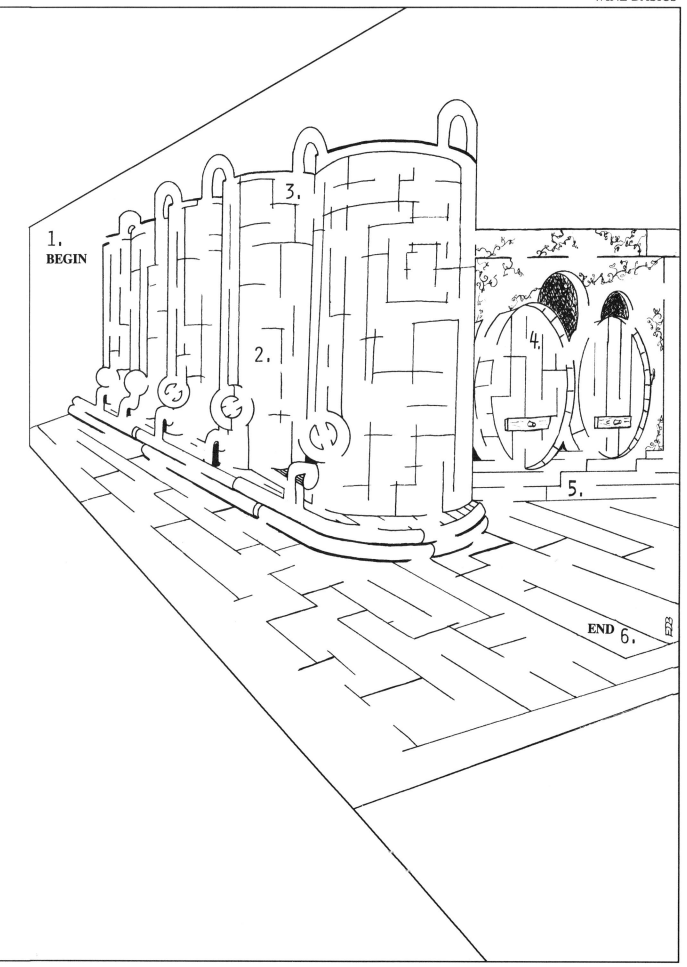

The Big O₂

The next 6 puzzles (#13 through #18) present some important facts on oxygen and wine. Oxygen is two-faced. It helps develop the wine, yet, eventually, it also helps to kill it. Play our puzzles and discover more.

13. Oxygen And Winemaking

Some non-wine words are scrambled up here. Help!

Sa wine si fermented, racked, and transferred, ti si coedhut dan dega a ttelli rome ceah mite by oxygen. Later, air trislef into het wine grotuhh hte cask's wood. After globitnt, any oxygen that senarim in the neiw is brodabes in a wef shnotm.

14. Oxygen And Heavy Wines

A simple (but informative!) substitution code. Need a clue? Look below.

JG B XJOF JT GVMM PG BMDPIPM, UBOOJO, TVHBS, BDJE, PS PUIFS TUSPOH JOHSFEJFOUT, JU OFFET UJNF UP CMFOE, TPGUFO, BOE CFDPNF B NBOZ – TQMFOEPSFE UIJOH.

XJOF MPWFST "MBZ EPXO" TVDI XJOFT GPS ZFBST (BOE EFDBEFT) VOUJM UIJT NBSSJBHF IBQQFOT. UIFO, PXOFST ESJOL UIFTF XJOFT CFGPSF PYZHFO PWFSNBUVSFT BOE TQPJMT UIFN.

FYBNQMFT: SFET - GJOF DMBSFUT, CVSHVOEJFT, BOE QPSU; XIJUFT – TBVUFSOFT, UIF CFTU HFSNBO SJFTMJOHT, BOE CVSHVOEJFT.

15. Oxygen and Light Wines

Five phrases in our maze form our message. Find those 5 phrases in order while you meander through the maze. Several paths lead you to 3 useless phrases, so read each phrase that you come to and see if it fits together with the other phrases and makes sense. If you enter through one door, you must exit through another. Our maze is inspired by the strong twine that used to hold down the stoppers in Champagne bottles. String along!

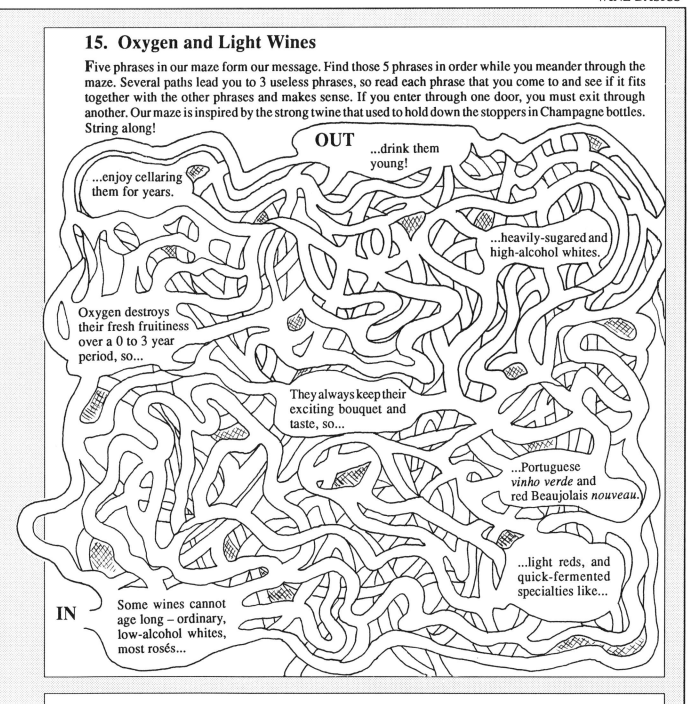

OUT

...drink them young!

...enjoy cellaring them for years.

...heavily-sugared and high-alcohol whites.

Oxygen destroys their fresh fruitiness over a 0 to 3 year period, so...

They always keep their exciting bouquet and taste, so...

...Portuguese *vinho verde* and red Beaujolais *nouveau.*

...light reds, and quick-fermented specialties like...

IN

Some wines cannot age long – ordinary, low-alcohol whites, most rosés...

16. Oxygen And Scent

Find three fragrant wine facts. Put Sentence A's words in order, then Sentence B's, then C's.

A. bouquet of also Slow enhances the oxidation the wine.

B. wine's and alcohol helps Oxidation fruit combine. to acid a

C. which lovely (compounds) creates off aromas. This give esters

17. Oxygen And Bottle Storage*

Store corked, bottled wine on its side to keep the cork wet...

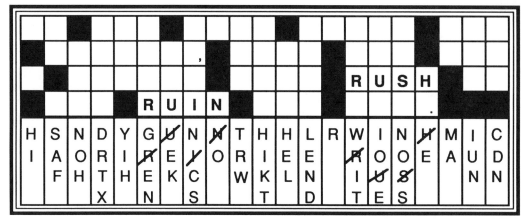

** To solve this kind of puzzle, put the letters in each vertical column into the boxes in the same column directly above them and make words. When you're finished, read **across the boxes** for our message. (Black boxes mark the ends of words.) We started you off with 2 helps.*

18. Oxygen And Serving

The words in each line are in order; the 12 lines themselves are not. Can you fix them?

1. DRINK. ONE PREFERRED WAY IS TO SPLASH THE

2. THE WHOLE BOTTLE CAN GET TOO WARM TO

3. "BREATHE" HELPS. SOME FOLKS LEAVE IT IN THE OPENED

4. SERVING. SO MUCH OXYGEN AT ONCE "OPENS" THE

5. "CLOSED" WINE AROUND IN THE GLASS TO AERATE IT.

6. EVER, AIR TOUCHES JUST THE TOP OF THE WINE, AND

7. MORE DRINKABLE. IN A RESTAURANT, KNOCK A

8. IF A WINE IS TOO YOUNG OR TOO

9. WINE, RELEASES THE BOUQUET, AND MAKES IT MUCH

10. ˙BOTTLE FOR 15 MINUTES TO SEVERAL HOURS. HOW-

11. WINE INTO A DECANTER OR CARAFE BEFORE

12. POWERFUL TO DRINK, SOMETIMES LETTING IT

19. Lines On Vines

Folks who are new to wine become fascinated with grapes, but they shamelessly neglect the grapes' vital staff of life – the vine. Below, our introduction to vine basics is filled with **26 bold-lettered** words. They'll be fun for you to find in our vineyard.

All grapes belong to the scientific **genus** *Vitis.* Grapes that make the world's most famous wines (Cabernet Sauvignon, Chardonnay, Pinot Noir, etc.) are of the ***Vitis vinifera*** species and **grow** well in Europe and the western U.S.

These *vinifera* varieties didn't flourish in many other U.S. regions, so winemakers in those areas relied on **native** American **species** such as the ***Vitis labrusca*** (which produces the **Concord** and Catawba grapes). Grapes from these native vines make wines with a grapey, **"foxy"** taste: because they are so different, many *vinifera* lovers don't like them. French-American hybrid **vines** aim to combine native hardiness and *vinifera* depth and taste: the Aurora and Seyval Blanc varieties are popular French-American **hybrids.**

Each vine type and its grapes have **unique soil** and weather needs, **yield** capacity, and best **use.** One type will produce **eating grapes** and **raisins**; another will make common wines; another very fine wines.

In the 1870's, the *phylloxera vastatrix* bug **destroyed** almost all of Europe's vineyards. Today, most *vinifera* vines in Europe and elsewhere are **grafted** onto American **rootstock**, much of which is **immune** to the hungry **pest**. However, the insect world is adaptable and **phylloxera** can find new vine weaknesses at any time. Also, in the 1980's, a desire to quickly start new vineyards led some California wineries to avoid grafting and to plant *vinifera* cuttings on their own roots. For these and other reasons, some outstanding grape areas are now modern **victims** of the *phylloxera* plague. In addition, a few Napa districts, plus Lodi, Paso Robles, and other California areas battle another vine nemesis, the *nematode.*

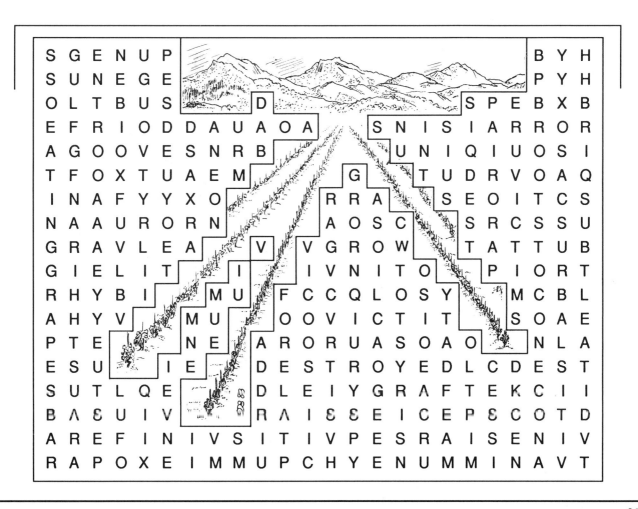

20. Great Grapes

The world's most appreciated wines come from the many different grape varieties of the *Vitis vinifera** species. Listed below are some famous *vinifera* grapes. On the facing page, we've described each grape. The trick here is to **match** each grape to its **Description**. If you can't guess them all, try this solution: grow the grapes in their proper grid spaces to give each of them a number. Then, transfer them by number to their **Descriptions**.

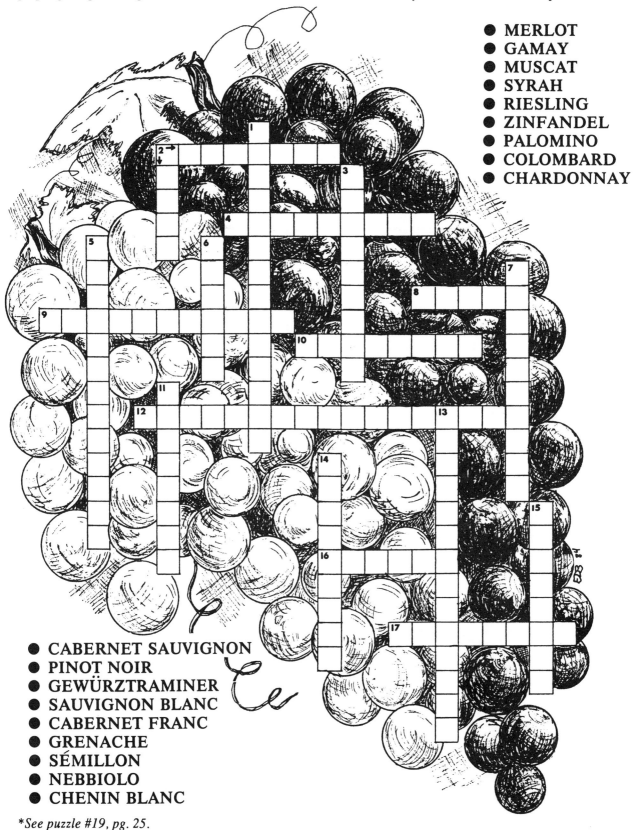

- MERLOT
- GAMAY
- MUSCAT
- SYRAH
- RIESLING
- ZINFANDEL
- PALOMINO
- COLOMBARD
- CHARDONNAY

- CABERNET SAUVIGNON
- PINOT NOIR
- GEWÜRZTRAMINER
- SAUVIGNON BLANC
- CABERNET FRANC
- GRENACHE
- SÉMILLON
- NEBBIOLO
- CHENIN BLANC

*See puzzle #19, pg. 25.

DESCRIPTIONS OF RED GRAPES

2 Down _____ The chief Beaujolais, France, grape. It makes fruity, fragrant red wines and lively California rosés.

2 Across _____ Blended into rosés and full reds in the French Rhône and Spanish Rioja areas, and into popular rosés and jug wines in California.

3. _____ A native of the U.S., Hungary, or Italy? No one's certain yet, but California claimed it and turns it into many kinds of light and full-bodied reds, whites, and rosés.

4. _____ Adds body to Champagne. France's Burgundy region forms great, velvety, agreeable wines from it and California and Oregon are starting to develop delicious ones.

5. _____ Used in California and France for pleasurable reds and rosés.

6. _____ Helps to form Bordeaux claret blends. California often adds wine made from this grape to soften its assertive Cabernet Sauvignon varietal wines.

8. _____ Favored in the Rhône region of France, then in Australia, and now in California, this grape makes potent red wines.

12. _____ This grape makes powerful reds that usually need wood and bottle aging.

15. _____ An Italian favorite, especially in Piedmont; it creates complex, ageable wines. California is growing it, too.

DESCRIPTIONS OF WHITE GRAPES

1. _____ Forms distinctive sweet and dry Bordeaux, Loire, and California wines. It is often blended with soft Grape #17, and is also known as *"Fumé Blanc."*

7. _____ This grape makes popular and important Champagne, white Burgundy, and dry California table wines. Folks used to mistakenly add *"Pinot"* to the front of this grape's name.

9. _____ Used in the Loire and California for fruity, textured, dry and sweetish wines.

10. _____ Called the greatest white; it's fashioned into perfumed, fruity, complex wines.

11. _____ Spain's main sherry grape.

13. _____ This grape's called "spicy," but many say it's really flowery.

14. _____ A main grape in California "Chablis;" well-liked as a fresh varietal.

16. _____ World-famous grape that's increasing in U.S. popularity. It has a black version, but wines are usually made from the white; forms grapey, fragrant wines.

17. _____ This grape and the #10 grape can develop *botrytis cinerea*, a fungus that lets water evaporate out of the grape: it concentrates grape sugar and flavors inside. Because this fungus fashions lush, succulent wines, many gratefully call it the "noble rot."

21. Soil And Climate

Each soil and climate of every country and region infuses its unique character, taste, and aroma into its grapes and wines. This game should give you a feel for some of the hundreds of vineyard conditions that can affect grapes and the wines they make. Ready?

What a mess! You know nothing about wine, but have just inherited vineyards. Sixteen reports on vineyard conditions have poured in. Your secretary condensed each report (See below?) but she scrambled 2 words in each condensation. **If you unscramble her 32 mistakes,** you can at least read the condensed versions below. **When you finish, hop to the facing page** and see another secretarial surprise.

1. Vineyards in north Europe and N.Y. State report that rain and cold are **plognisi** blossoms and fruit set. This will retard sugar and yeast **pledveemton.**

2. Clay soil = poor drainage. Hope for light **lirflana** so that the vine roots don't **treaglow** and spoil grape quality.

3. Grapes can't **trueam** as perfectly in your **stroahent** vineyards as they do on the slightly sunnier hills facing south.

4. Chalk soil **cefsterl** light onto your grapes – they should make **gleetna** wines, if the weather holds.

5. Volcanic soil characterizes this vineyard; your wines may show a "mineral" **feartettsa.** Some folks say that this is just in the **aingantimoi.**

6. Wines from your flat vineyards may not be as fine as those from your **lewl-dearidn, plesdo** ones.

7. **martsHloi!** This vineyard is ruined. Collect on your hail **esnicaunr** – you paid enough for it.

8. Slate soil here adds "**letes**" to your wine's taste – also fuller bouquet to its smell. Some say this idea is **lylis.**

9. Lucky!! Winds off of the river warm your vines **githllys** more than they warm your neighbors' vines. Your grapes have an **veatdnaga.**

10. Early spring frost **criedtpde.** Heat vines with smoke blankets and stoves – maybe spray them with water: its icy shell can save vines from frost **tadsesri.**

11. Too much spring rain. Your **wrilnefgo** fruit is destroyed. September rains expected – **widlme** could ruin the vines.

12. Damp **rawheet** assists the fuzzy *botrytis cinerea** mold to grow on your **omSnélil** grapes. Mmmmm. The wine will be rich and flavorsome.

13. Soil in this vineyard is too **lifteer.** Vines that **greltgus** for existence often make wines with better bouquet and taste sensations.

14. Too much sun. Grapes could **prein** early, and lose **theccraar** and bouquet.

15. Vineyard in hot climate – grape acid is **ceedadres** – wines can have less bouquet and finesse. You can fashion sweet dessert wines or use modern **trinefogreari** to help create table wines.

16. **vlearG** soil = good drainage. Wines send roots deep to form fine acid/sugar **cleabna** in the grapes and wines.

For more about botrytis, see Puzzle # 20, p. 27.

After your secretary condensed those reports, she left the originals on the floor! Try to find a path from the bottom of the page through all these papers and symbols and go to lunch.

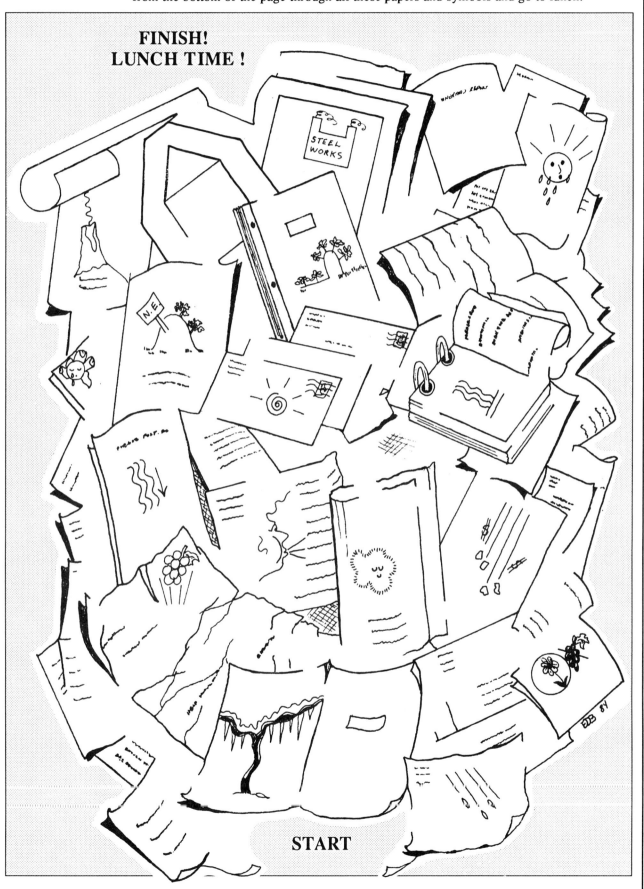

FINISH!
LUNCH TIME !

START

22. The Smells Of Wine

Appreciating scent is vital to wine enjoyment. A wine's scent can reveal its age, grape type, kind of sugar, alcohol, origin, soil, climate, additives, treatment, barrel wood type, etc. The **BOLD** words below describe some wine smells. These words also stand ready to reveal themselves in the *amphora* on the opposite page. **Can you circle them all?**

APPLEY............................ An apple-type aroma in young wines comes from malic acid.

AROMA............................ Describes the simple smell of a single fruit in younger wine – "an aroma of blackberries," "a Gewürztraminer aroma." Usually loses its strength with age.

BOUQUET........................ A mature wine gives off several smells. Bouquet refers to their total effect on the drinker's nose.

BUTTERY......................... Often a result of malolactic fermentation, a second fermentation that reduces a wine's fruity crispness and softens and rounds it.

COMPLEX........................ The wine may suggest to the nose many overlapping aromas. For example, one wine might bring to mind chocolate, cherries, pine, and tarragon.

FLINTY............................ A smell like that of flint sparks; often noted in French Chablis.

FOXY................................ Distinct, gamy scent of wine made from native American, non-*vinifera* grapes.

GREEN, STALKY, STEMMY........................ Sometimes this sharp scent adds crispness, but it can be overdone. It might be due to underripe grapes or immature vines.

HONEY............................ A scent found in some fine sweet wines.

LIVELY, FLOWERY...... Usually used to describe wine with an attractive, fresh scent.

NOSE................................ People use this general term to denote either bouquet or aroma or both.

OAK.................................. Oak barrels and (sneaky move) oak chips give other flavor aspects to wine. Some folks love a strong oak smell; others think that such an aroma means that the winemaker is either careless or a carpenter.

STALE.............................. This "off" odor is sometimes evident right after opening the bottle. Dissipate it by moving the wine around in the glass.

SULPHURY...................... This "burning" smell causes the drinker's nose to recoil. It can be from leftover sulphur used in winemaking. Ugh.

VANILLA.......................... One of the scents that an oak cask can give to a wine.

VEGGIE........................... A smell of asparagus or other vegetable instead of the smell of grape or fruit. Often due to overwatered or overfertilized grapes.

YEASTY........................... A (sometimes pleasant) fresh bread smell in the wine. It may mean that the wine is poorly made or that it's still fermenting. Some winemakers maintain that it's a normal smell from leaving the wine on the lees, or fermentation residue.

DAFFY DEFINITION: Cabernet - a stage musical and movie set in pre-WW II Germany. Its most famous song includes the phrase, "...life is a Cabernet," but critics agree that neither production used wine effectively. Two thumbs down, wine-wise.

Ancient Greeks and Romans stored some of their wine in *amphorae*.* These were pointed, 2-handled earthenware containers that stood upright inside metal holders and hollowed-out countertops. They were easily pushed into wet sand to keep their contents cool.

Amphorae is the plural of *amphora*. Modern folks just say, "amphoras."

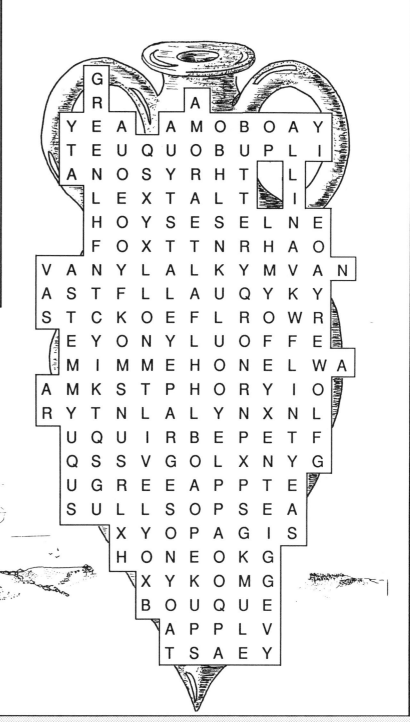

```
        G           A
    Y E A   A M O B O A Y
    T E U Q U O B U P L I
    A N O S Y R H T L L I
    L E X T A L T L I N E
    H O Y S E S E L N E O
    F O X T T N R H A O
V A N Y L A L K Y M V A N
A S T F L L A U Q Y K Y
S T C K O E F L R O W R
E Y O N Y L U O F F E
M I M M E H O N E L W A
A M K S T P H O R Y I O
R Y T N L A L Y N X N L
U Q U I R B E P E T F
Q S S V G O L X N Y G
U G R E E A P P T E
S U L L S O P S E A
    X Y O P A G I S
    H O N E O K G
    X Y K O M G G
    B O U Q U E
    A P P L V
    T S A E Y
```

QUESTION. Someone who places her hand over a glass, swirls the wine around inside, then sticks her nose into the glass, sniffing deeply, is:

      A. showing off.

      B. a genuine wine appreciator who knows how to experience wine.

ANSWER: Could be either.

23. The Looks Of Wine

Oenophiles (wine lovers) challenge themselves to describe a wine's precise appearance. Below, we've listed wine shades and visual qualities found both alone and layered in the glass. (A fine wine usually displays several colors.) See if you can place all the **BOLD** words in their correct boxes below.

<u>3 Letters</u>: **RED**

<u>4 Letters</u>: **BLUE, GOLD, LIME, PINK, ROSE, RUBY, LEGS** (*Legs* are streamers that cling to the inside of a tilted wine glass. They're formed from the glycerine in a fine wine.)

<u>5 Letters</u>: **AMBER, BRICK, CLEAR, GREEN, HONEY, LEMON, STRAW, TAWNY, WHITE, BROWN** (*Brown* is fine in Madeira or sherry. In other wines, it can indicate overaging.)

<u>6 Letters</u>: **ALMOND, BUTTER, GARNET, ORANGE, PURPLE, YELLOW, CLOUDY** (A wine can be cloudy for good and bad reasons. Some winemakers prefer to make unfiltered wine, which can be cloudy.)

<u>8 Letters</u>: **MARIGOLD, BLACKISH** (A black cast might be due to heavy tannin in the wine.)

<u>9 Letters</u>: **ONIONSKIN, RASPBERRY, MADERIZED** (The term *maderized* means that the wine is brown with too much age.)

DAFFY DEFINITION: Maderized – made even angrier.

24. The Tastes Of Wine

Firms are changing their wine stoppers and caps to hold down expense, to keep lead away from the wine, and to prevent "corked" wine (wine spoiled by corks that acquire unwanted chemicals in processing). If plastic and non-lead metal stoppers don't affect the wine's taste or chemistry, they'll be used more and more on wine products. While we still have them, look among the corks* below for our 18 **BOLD** terms. These terms describe the flavors and sensations of wine in the mouth.

ACID.................................. Tasted especially on the inside of the lips and tongue tip. In wine, it's best when balanced – just to give a crispness – and not overpowering.

APPLEY............................. An apple tang in light white wines comes from the wines' malic acid.

BAKED, TOASTED.......... The result of the hot sun on grapes, or of heat used in the wine's making.

COARSE, ROUGH........... These name a poorly-made wine whose qualities don't blend together.

DRY.................................... The opposite of sweet.

EXPERIENCE.................. Your own experience tells you, the expert, what you like.

FRUITY............................ Describes a fresh sense of the main grape in the wine.

HARSH, HARD................. A sensation often due to tannin.

LONG FINISH................. This phrase denotes the wine's aftertaste that lingers in the mouth.

SHORT FINISH............... The opposite of a long finish; flavor quickly disappears off the tongue.

SLURP.............................. After swirling and smelling the wine, draw some into your mouth; touch it everywhere inside. Through your pursed lips, drag air into your mouth and let it act on the wine before swallowing it. If you slurp while trying this, enjoy it.

SOFT................................. The wine imparts a plush sensation and is non-aggressive in the mouth.

SWEET.............................. Come on. You know you don't need a definition for "sweet."

TANNIN............................ This component puckers the mouth, especially the sides of the tongue and cheeks.

YEASTY............................ This taste of fresh bread often means that the wine is poorly made; perhaps it wasn't cleansed of yeast particles, or is still fermenting.

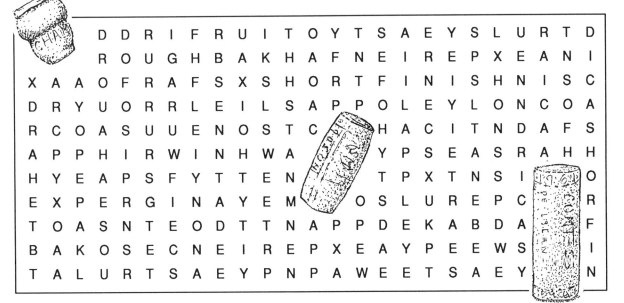

*The best natural corks come from the **Quercus suber** trees in Portugal and Spain. Make them feel at home.*

25. Bureau Of Bottle Investigation

We've set up a few popular wine bottles below. Can you match each **Bottle Shape** to its **Bottle Description** on the opposite page? If you can't complete our match-up, try our **Character Match-Up**. If **Character #1** matches **Character Description "A"**, then **Bottle Shape #1** will match **Bottle Description "A."**

BOTTLE SHAPES

1. 2. 3. 4. 5. 6.

7. 8. 9. 10.

New News! Bottle changes are in the works. French and U.S. winemakers and U.C. Davis are investigating "light-struck" wines. Wines regularly suffer a speedy decline in taste after spending only short periods of time in natural sunlight or under fluorescent lighting. Bottles with ultraviolet protection or deep amber color may soon replace today's clear and lightly tinted bottles.

DAFFY DEFINITION: Magnum – A wine bottle shaped like Tom Selleck. Sales are good.

BOTTLE DESCRIPTIONS

A. **Bordeaux.** The world's most popular shape for red and white wines holds 750 milliliters (25.4 oz.) It is shouldered and straight-sided; Bordeaux uses green glass for red wines and clear glass for the whites. Finer Chianti wine from Tuscany, Italy – *Chianti Classico* – goes into this type of bottle.

B. The famous straw-covered **Chianti Fiasco** contains 1 liter (33.8 oz.) of everyday red wine. Italian Orvieto whites use a smaller version.

C. **Champagne** bottles are slope-shouldered, like Burgundy bottles. However, they are made thicker than regular wine bottles to withstand the powerful CO_2 pressure inside.

D. The **Champagne Magnum** holds the equivalent of 2 regular champagne bottles. Some believe that Champagne tastes best out of this larger bottle.

E. New! Two-thirds the size (500 milliliters) of the standard 750 milliliter bottle. Merlion, Jordan, and other wineries aim this **half-liter** size at diners who want more than a glass and less than a bottle.

F. The slender, shoulderless **Rhine** (or **German**) wine bottles are colored green for Mosel wines and brown for other German wines. French wines from Alsace use the green version of this bottle.

G. The brown, **Traditional Port** bottle has a bulbous neck. This allows its long cork to expand and perform well during long aging.

H. Besides the traditional port bottle, Portugal also uses this **Long-Necked Port** shape.

I. The **Franconian Bocksbeutel** is a famous holder for the white wines of the Franken region in Germany. Chile also uses it for its Riesling wines.

J. This slope-shouldered **Burgundy** bottle is used all over the world for reds and whites. It is usually made of green glass. Italy's Piedmont, Barolo, and Barbera wines use this type in a brown color.

CHARACTER MATCH-UP (In case you're stuck)
Remember, what matches here also matches above.

CHARACTER NAMES	CHARACTER DESCRIPTIONS
1. Casper	A. Mel Blanc's wisecracker
2. Tweety Bird	B. Jealous of #8.
3. Donald Duck	C. Tot he taw...
4. Mighty Mouse	D. "Back Off!"
5. Mr. Magoo	E. Husky rodent
6. Yogi Bear	F. Daisy's guy
7. Daffy Duck	G. Friendly frightener
8. Bugs Bunny	H. Ranger's nemesis
9. Yosemite Sam	I. Glasses, please
10. Little Lulu	J. Annie's friend

26. Glasses – Global And Glorious

Effective wine glasses enhance the wines they're made to hold. Centuries of development have produced some favorite wine glass styles. Can you match these famous **Glass Styles** to their **Descriptions**? If you'd like a helping hand, play our **Character Match-Up**. If **Character Name #1** matches **Character Description "A,"** then **Glass Style #1** will match **Glass Description "A."**

GLASS STYLES

DAFFY DEFINITION: Hock Glass – a crystal goblet highly prized by German pawn shops.

GLASS DESCRIPTIONS

A. The **Basic Clear** style is the most serviceable all-purpose glass. It is used in sizes from 8 to 12 oz. and in 3 shapes – U-shaped, rounded, and rounded tulip. Fill its large bowl 1/3 to 2/3 full, so you can swirl the wine and free the bouquet: the curves of the glass channel the scent to your nose. The rounded, circular version is often associated with Burgundy reds and is called a "Paris Goblet."

B. The specialized **cognac** glass allows you to cup and warm the wine with your hands. Its bowl narrows at the top to capture vapors.

C. This tall regional glass from **Alsace**, France has a clear glass bowl and a green glass stem. The stem reflects its color into the region's white wines. It's used in the German Mosel region, too.

D. A shallow, squared-off bowl characterizes the traditional glass from the **Anjou** region, in the French Loire River area.

E. The British use the word *hock* to describe German Rhine wines. **Hock** glasses can be highly decorated, often with ornate brown glass stems.

F. The slender, serviceable **Copita** for sherry means "little mouthful." Fill it half-full.

G. The cuts in **Engraved Mosel** wine glasses spark light into white wines from Germany's Mosel River.

H. **Sparkling wine and Champagne** glasses prolong the bubbles by keeping air away from the wine. Some ideal glass shapes for bubbly wines are trumpet, elongated balloon, and flute. The flat 'traditional' wedding glasses and glasses that are fully rounded let too much air touch the wine.

I. Today, wine glass innovation goes on. Perhaps new designs will inspire future wine glass traditions. This is a **taster's glass** from creator Jacques Pascot. (His line is called "*Les Impitoyables.*")

CHARACTER MATCH-UP (In case you're stuck)

Remember, what matches here also matches above.

CHARACTER NAMES	CHARACTER DESCRIPTIONS
1. Wile E.	A. Suffers in the desert
2. Mickey	B. Wants that wascally wabbit
3. Elmer	C. Tha-that's his trademark
4. Porky	D. Craves a yellow mouthful
5. Chilly Willy	E. Disney's first
6. Sylvester	F. Loves the South
7. Woody	G. Mr. Lantz's bird
8. Felix	H. Psychiatrist
9. Lucy	I. Has a bag of tricks

27. Once Upon A Time

He who knows the past is wiser about the present. Explore wine ages past: solve our crossword, then transfer the words by number to the blanks on the facing page. Our design of vines trained into a bower is from one of many wine pictures in the tomb of the Egyptian official, Nakht (c. 1300 B.C.).

ACROSS

2. A boat's front sail
4. The start of animals
5. Brief regulation
6. Catches flies in the outfield
10. Wine prefix from the Greek
11. National for short
12. Sneaked
16. Maui dance
17. Norway's patron saint
18. Used to be
19. Districts
23. Purpose
24. "Do it or ____!"
25. Hardens

DOWN

1. *The Great ____ Adventure*
2. Containers
3. Hank's movie
6. Musical creation
7. Cure
8. Poker admission
9. Midas' metal

12. Presentations
13. A donkey and mare cross
14. End of singular
15. Presented
19. The Middle ____
20. Part to play
21. The Far ____
22. Malt beers

An unearthed French grape leaf fossil 12D_____ that grapes and vines are 19D_____ (at least 60 million years) old. Man began cultivating them around 6000 B.C. in the Mesopotamian and the Caspian Sea 19A_____. By 3000 B.C., Egypt and Phoenicia enjoyed 1D_____; and by 2000 B.C. the Greek islands 18A_____ famous for it.

Early mankind recorded in 6D_____, story, and inventories the vital 20D_____ that 1D_____ played in life: wine's creation was mysterious; it could 7D_____ and calm; its vines grew where little 24A_____ grew; and it 15D_____ raisins and shade. An ancient vineyard was a possession as good as 9D_____.

The first named biblical vintner was Noah, and the Old Testament repeatedly praises the vine. Joshua and Caleb's 23A_____ was to scout and spy on Canaan. They 12A_____ out a huge grape cluster as proof of the land's riches.

The 3D_____ cellars of the Assyrian kings flourished. The navigating Phoenicians spread vine cultivation from the Middle 21D_____ throughout the Mediterranean. The Egyptians' god, Osiris, brought them the vine and their tombs picture every aspect of winemaking.

The ancients transported 1D_____ in animal skins and they protected open 1D_____ 2D_____ from air with a layer of oil on top. To drink these wines, they diluted them with water, then stirred in combinations of honey, spices, herbs, perfumes, and flowers.

DAFFY DEFINITION: Joshua and Caleb – patrons of people who, even in the face of danger, seize opportunities to share wine.

28. It's Greek To Me

Travel back in time and share Greece's ancient wine. Solve our crossword, then transfer the words by number to the blanks on the facing page.

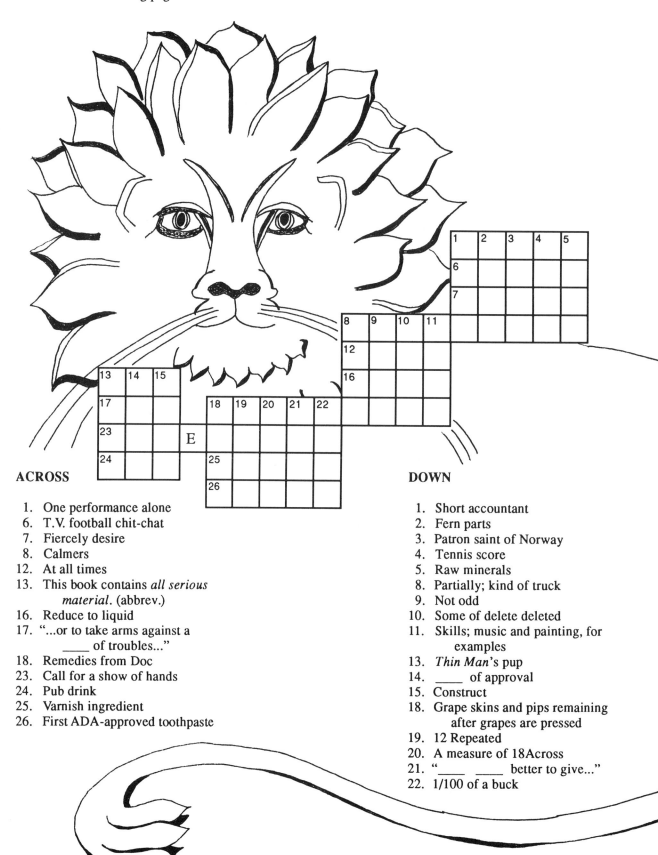

ACROSS

1. One performance alone
6. T.V. football chit-chat
7. Fiercely desire
8. Calmers
12. At all times
13. This book contains *all serious material*. (abbrev.)
16. Reduce to liquid
17. "...or to take arms against a _____ of troubles..."
18. Remedies from Doc
23. Call for a show of hands
24. Pub drink
25. Varnish ingredient
26. First ADA-approved toothpaste

DOWN

1. Short accountant
2. Fern parts
3. Patron saint of Norway
4. Tennis score
5. Raw minerals
8. Partially; kind of truck
9. Not odd
10. Some of delete deleted
11. Skills; music and painting, for examples
13. *Thin Man*'s pup
14. _____ of approval
15. Construct
18. Grape skins and pips remaining after grapes are pressed
19. 12 Repeated
20. A measure of 18 Across
21. "_____ _____ better to give..."
22. 1/100 of a buck

Greece started its viticulture around 2000 B.C. **12A**_____ since Homer (who lived around the tenth **22D**_____. B.C.) said, "Wine gives strength to the weary man," the Greeks continued to write about it. Aristotle's pupil Theophrastus (*287 B.C.*), and the globetrotting Herodotus (*400 B.C.*) advised on the **11D**_____ of planting vines and making wine. Virgil (*30 B.C.*) coined another popular wine phrase with "Vines **4D**_____ an open hill."

The cult of Dionysus,* god of wine, arose in Asia and grew into the Greek drama and drinking festival, the *Dionysia*. In everyday life, Greek dinner guests made a game of flinging the last drops of wine in their cups at a target dish.

Wines also served as **8A**_____ and **18A**_____. The Greeks cooked their wines and diluted them with hot water to **15D**_____ them **8D**_____ – strength and light in **6A**_____. A **20D** _____ of Greek wine also had fruit and herbs blended into it. **21D**_____ _____ a mystery to modern drinkers just how the ancient Greeks could ever **7A**_____ such wine. But then, as (especially) now, every society develops its own taste preferences.

Between 600 and 200 B.C., the Greeks invented the beam press, crossed the Mediterranean **17A**_____ , and planted vineyards in southern France. They'd also **16A**_____ **25A**_____ to **14D**_____ their porous earthen wine vessels (*amphorae*). And, **9D**_____ today, Greek *Retsina* wine has the same **25A**_____ flavor.

* *Traditionally, Dionysus (dye-uh-NYE-suss) is often pictured with a stylized dolphin or a lion (like the one decorating these pages).*

29. When In Rome

Find out what wine things those Romans were up to! **Finish our crossword, then transfer the words by number to the spaces on the facing page.** You'll also read about our puzzle illustration, which is based on a 4th century Roman mosaic.

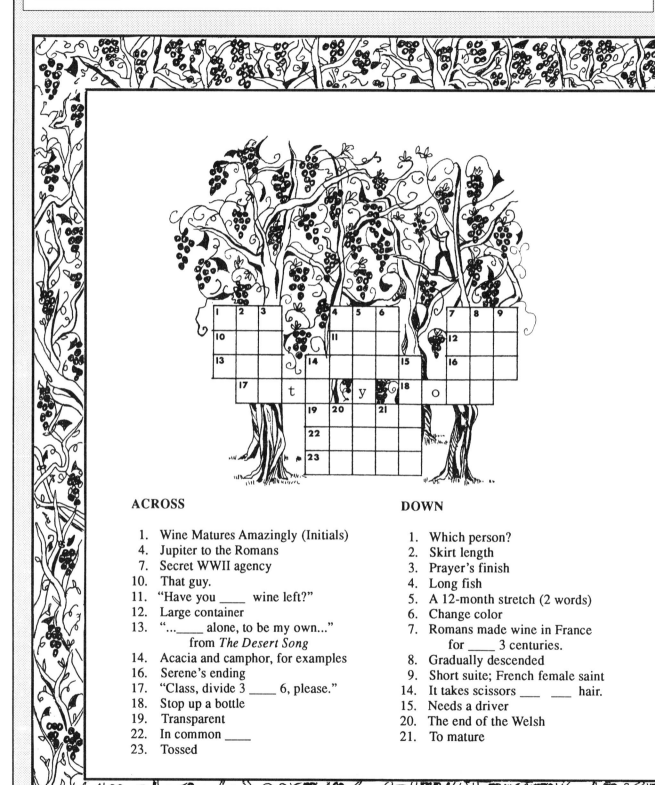

ACROSS

1. Wine Matures Amazingly (Initials)
4. Jupiter to the Romans
7. Secret WWII agency
10. That guy.
11. "Have you _____ wine left?"
12. Large container
13. "..._____ alone, to be my own..."
    from *The Desert Song*
14. Acacia and camphor, for examples
16. Serene's ending
17. "Class, divide 3 _____ 6, please."
18. Stop up a bottle
19. Transparent
22. In common _____
23. Tossed

DOWN

1. Which person?
2. Skirt length
3. Prayer's finish
4. Long fish
5. A 12-month stretch (2 words)
6. Change color
7. Romans made wine in France
    for _____ 3 centuries.
8. Gradually descended
9. Short suite; French female saint
14. It takes scissors ___ ___ hair.
15. Needs a driver
20. The end of the Welsh
21. To mature

The Romans turned Dionysus, the Greek wine and drama deity, **17A**_____ Bacchus, an earthy, drunken **2D**_____ – **4A**_____. Celebrations in honor of **10A**_____ **8D**_____ **17A**_____ riotous orgies which **5D**_____ _____ (186 B.C.) were finally banned.

But vines and winemaking increased. Rome **23A**_____ her troops into action. They moved along major waterways, and continued **14D**_____ _____ new vineyards **17A**_____ the lands they conquered. By the 4th century, Roman vineyards dotted Portugal, Spain, the French regions of Burgundy, Loire, and Champagne, and the German Mosel and Rhine river basins.

The **15D**_____ press, **18A**_____ stoppers (from Spanish and Portuguese **18A**_____ **14A**_____), and the use of bottles allowed the Romans to save and to **21D**_____ their wines. (Most bottle and **18A**_____ **22A**_____ disappeared with the Roman Empire.) Romans used egg whites to "fine," or **19A**_____, wine and they copied the Celts' wooden **12A**_____ and cask to store and transport it.

13A_____ Roman custom, that of training vines **7D**_____ **11A**_____ tall **14A**_____, survives today in south Italy and northern Portugal. Like the Greeks, the Romans added water, spices, and herbs to their wine.

30. Hot (Historical) Flashes!

We have uncovered some old (very old) news releases that once announced **great wine milestones!** You, too, can share these amazing news flashes! Place the words below into their correct boxes, then transfer them by number to the spaces on the facing page! Live once again those thrilling days of yesteryear!

2 LETTERS: BE

3 LETTERS: ALL, ART, ASS, HIS, YET

4 LETTERS: BEST, CORK, HILL, INNS, LIME, NAVY, THEY

5 LETTERS: AGING, CASKS, CURSE, EVERY, GOING, GRAFT, LOUSE, RHINE, SPRAY, TELLS, TOURS, VINES

6 LETTERS: COPPER, EUROPE, GRISON, IMMUNE, IMPORT, MARTIN, MILDEW, OIDIUM, SEASON, TONNES

7 LETTERS: BOTTLES, CENTERS, DISEASE, FAILING, PIRATES, PRUNING, TONNAGE

8 LETTERS: AMERICAN, BLENDING, BORDEAUX, LABRUSCA, LEARNING, PÉRIGNON, SULPHATE, VINIFERA

9 LETTERS: CHAMPAGNE, ROOTSTOCK

10 LETTERS: PHYLLOXERA

11 LETTERS: CHARLEMAGNE, MONASTERIES

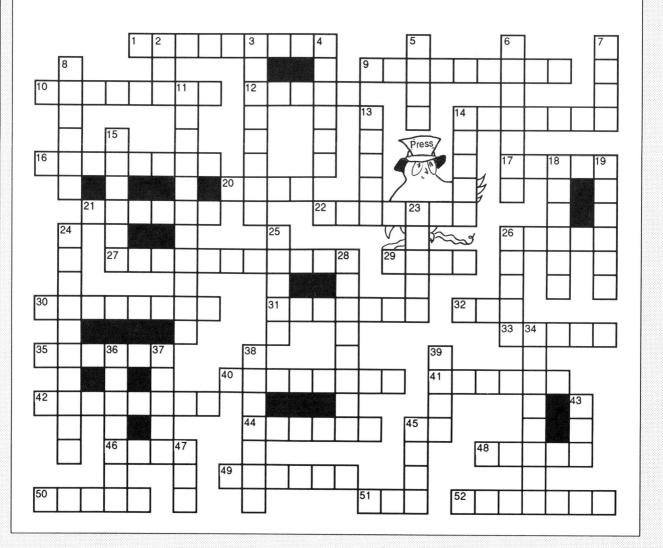

360 A.D........FLASH! Saint (8_____ of (26A_____ notes that the grape (48_____ munched by an (43_____ last (49_____ are producing more grapes now. "I call it (52'_____'," says Marty.

Dark
Ages.........FLASH! (27_____, acting as (7_____ and (42_____ (14A_____, keep viticulture (17_____. Bravo, Padres!

800's.............FLASH! Yesterday, (11_____ saw that the Johannisberg (29_____ on the (37_____ loses its snow before (32_____ the others and ordered it planted with grape (48_____. The court press release states, "If it's the (45D_____ (29_____ now, it will (47_____ (45A_____ the (45D_____ 1100 years from now."

1200's..........FLASH! Now that England rules Bordeaux and southern France, it wants to (41_____ French wine. Her ships are arming against wine (36_____. Some say this is the start of a real British (20_____!
Additional Flash: The amount of (44_____, or huge wine (13_____ a ship can carry, now designates her size. You'll hear the word (6 "_____" a lot from now on.

1500's..........FLASH! MEXICO! Some weird minds in Cortez's fun-loving Mex-Conquer Division decided to (25_____ their European vines to native ones! Those crazies claim that a native root-killing (50_____, the (24_____, may kill European vines, but it doesn't ruin native (9_____. We love ya', you wild guys!

Late
1600's.........FLASH! Dom (34_____, cellar master, Hautvillers Abbey, France, was honored today for single-handedly capturing bubbles inside (1_____, mastering the (51_____ of (30_____ fine wines, and rediscovering the lost (5_____. The blind monk asserts that other winemakers also deserve credit. The beloved cleric expressed his concern, worried that (46_____ won't (45A_____ remembered. What modesty!

Same
Era.........FLASH! England's stronger (38_____, along with the (5_____, start the new fad of bottle – (23_____ fine wines.

1840's
and 50's....FLASH! (15_____, a powdery (21_____, turns grapes sickly: (48_____ (32_____ over (4_____ are (31_____!

Same
Time.........FLASH! Botanist A. M. (19_____'s (33_____ kills the (15_____ (22_____! Instinct (26D_____ us that even 20th century growers will dust vines with a form of (2_____ (33_____. Future generations might call it (40 "_____ Mixture," a blend of (35_____ (28_____ and weakened (39_____.

1880's.............FLASH! Since sneaking to France 20 years ago on (3_____ (48_____, the (14D_____ of (24_____ has destroyed fortunes and nearly (12_____ vineyard in Europe!

Same
Era.............FLASH! Shades of Cortez! As the noble Spanish did 300 years ago, scientists are rooting up almost all the European *vitis* (16_____ vines and grafting each one onto the roots of *vitis* (10_____ and other (18_____ native (3_____ (48_____. European winemaking is saved!

Wine And Food

The next 4 puzzles (Puzzles #31 through #34) explore wine as a companion to food. It's delicious when a wine matches its accompanying food: it's perfect when the food matches the chosen wine! There are traditional wine-and-food rules and there are exceptions to wine-and-food rules. You'll find some of both in these puzzles.

31. Ground Rules

This basic formula for tasting and serving wines has held up through the years and is designed to let taste and smell sensations awaken gradually. *(Directions are with Puzzle #14, pg. 24.)*

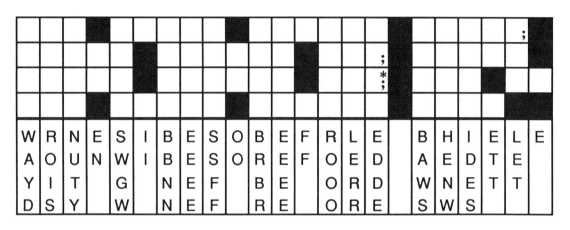

Letter bank:

W	R	N	E	S	I	B	E	S	O	B	E	F	R	L	E		B	H	I	E	L	E
A	O	U	N	W	I	B	E	S	O	R	E	F	O	E	D		A	E	D	T	T
Y	I	T		G		N	E	F		B	E		O	R	D		W	N	E	S	T	T
D	S	Y		W		N	E	F		R	E		O	R	E		S	W	S

* Except sweet whites. It's hard to appreciate a dry red wine after tasting a sweet white.

32. Ground Rules Broken

However, when someone says that a certain wine rule is unchangeable, or that it has no exceptions, keep in mind this quote given to us by master winemaker Joe Heitz of Heitz Cellars, Napa...

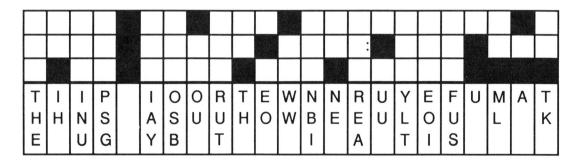

Letter bank:

T	I	I	P		I	O	O	R	T	E	W	N	N	R	U	Y	E	F	U	M	A	T
H	H	N	S		A	S	U	U	H	O	W	B	E	E	U	L	O	U			L		K
E		U	G		Y	B		T	T			I		A		T	I	S	S

33. Main Courses and Wine

Rustle up some helpful hints! Fit our **Words** into the grid below. Then, by number, fill in the blanks.

Words: **blend, compliment, different, dishes, dry, ham, light, medium, overpower, pleasant, pork, red, roasted, salmon, turkey, types, veal, white, wine**

You'll see many articles and recipes that upset the renowned rule, "Serve (7_____

(18_____ with fish; serve (2_____ (18_____ with meat." No matter the wine's color,

the wine and food shouldn't (5_____ each other: they should (1_____

and (9_____ with each other. So, you can enjoy a (7_____ or a (11_____

(2_____ with some (15_____ and (19_____ (6_____ dishes;

you might serve a (8_____ (16_____ (7_____ or a (13_____,

(8_____ (2_____ with (10_____ and roast (4_____; you may choose a full

(7_____ (such as white Zinfandel), or a big, fruity (2_____ (such as red Zinfandel), with

(17_____ (14_____ of (12_____ dishes, depending on their sauces.

Now *that we've looked at main dishes, turn the page and explore wine and other foods in Puzzle #34.*

34. Side Issues

Play with a few other interesting wine and food facts. Unscramble the **23 BOLD**, mixed-up words and phrases below, then have fun finding them in the wordfind.

Remember, the wine **LSOUDH** blend with all the food into a **SLIPGENA** whole. Strong seasonings, **GREVNIA**, **SUHMY** types of vegetables, horseradish, **SNOONI**, **SCRITU** fruits, and other foods can **HSLAC** with a fine wine.

One food and wine rule that has **PONSITXEEC** to it is the one that states, "Chocolate coats the tongue and hides a wine's flavor." An answer to that is to pair **ETWES** dessert Muscats with **HILTG** chocolate **SECKOIO** or mousses. Also, try savoring rich ports with triple-chocolate cake.

Even **UMSAOF** winemakers indulge in "unclassy" wine **THASIB**. They toss **CIE BECSU** into fine wine, and thoroughly **JYONE** a $3 bottle of wine with **PILSEM** food, for example.

You, too, should feel free to use **VIPEXNEES** and **AHPEC** wines in any way you like. But don't **SLEETT** on "pop" wines and coolers forever – you'll miss too much. A **IFEMETIL** of tasting growth and **USLAPERE** awaits you. **OG ROF TI**!

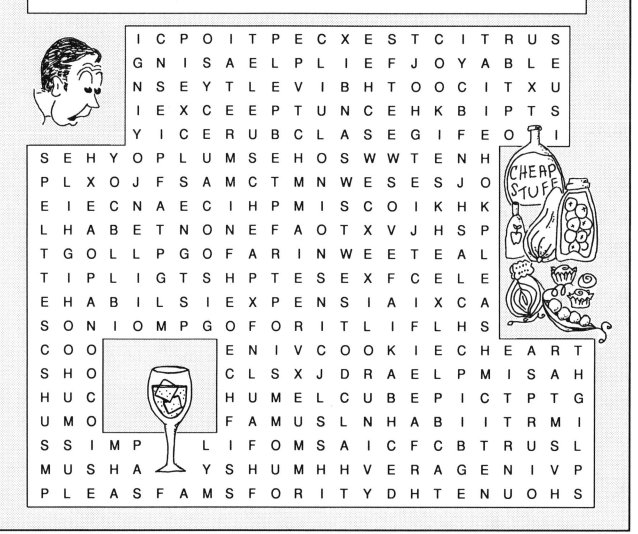

```
I C P O I T P E C X E S T C I T R U S
G N I S A E L P L I E F J O Y A B L E
N S E Y T L E V I B H T O O C I T X U
I E X C E E P T U N C E H K B I P T S
Y I C E R U B C L A S E G I F E O I
S E H Y O P L U M S E H O S W W T E N H
P L X O J F S A M C T M N W E S E S J O
E I E C N A E C I H P M I S C O I K H K
L H A B E T N O N E F A O T X V J H S P
T G O L L P G O F A R I N W E E T E A L
T I P L I G T S H P T E S E X F C E L E
E H A B I L S I E X P E N S I A I X C A
S O N I O M P G O F O R I T L I F L H S
C O O          E N I V C O O K I E C H E A R T
S H O       C L S X J D R A E L P M I S A H
H U C       H U M E L C U B E P I C T P T G
U M O       F A M U S L N H A B I I T R M I
S S I M P    L I F O M S A I C F C B T R U S L
M U S H A    Y S H U M H H V E R A G E N I V P
P L E A S F A M S F O R I T Y D H T E N U O H S
```

II. Wine Travels

Tours of Wine Regions and Methods In
California

with *Side Excursions* To
Oregon, Washington, New York, France,
Germany, Italy, Spain, Portugal, Australia,
and South America

Tickets ready?

Let's go!

35. California Conquest

Welcome to the Golden State and its nearly 800 wineries. California's wine areas can be divided by temperature zones, by geology, and by geography. The 7 popular (but imperfect) geographical divisions that are used most often are on our map – but 6 of them are scrambled! Get acquainted with these 6 wine **REGIONS** by **unscrambling them and placing their names on the correct blanks opposite**. Then, go on and play the puzzle at the bottom of the opposite page. California, here we come!

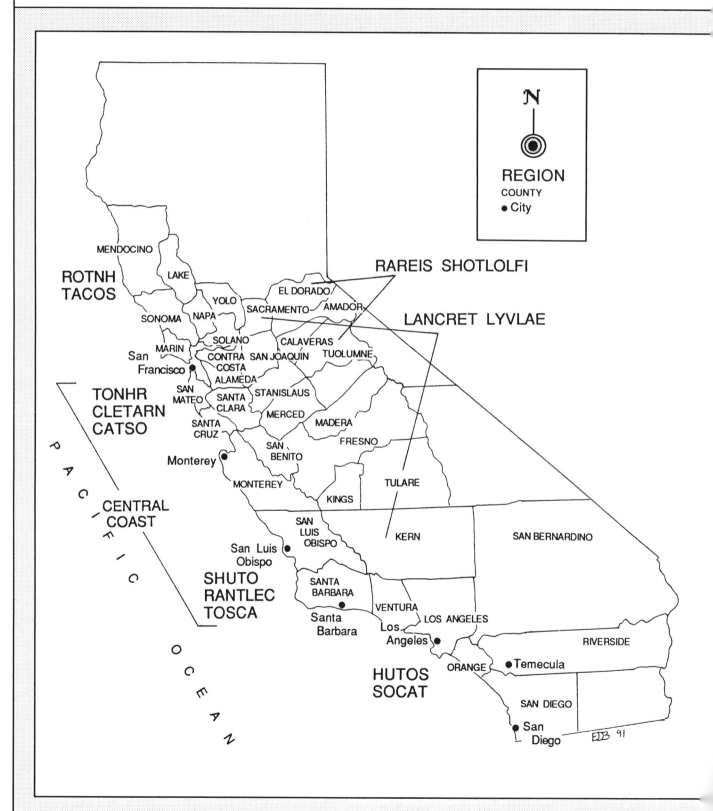

California's Six Main Geographic Wine Regions

A. — — — — ☐10 — — — ☐7 —

White grapes predominate in this area formed from Los Angeles, Ventura, San Bernardino, Riverside, and San Diego counties. It includes the burgeoning Temecula district.

B. — — — — ☐3 — ☐4 — — — — — — — — ☐8

With a solid and increasing reputation for excellence, this region contains the Bay Area counties of Contra Costa, Alameda (home of the Livermore Valley), and San Mateo, plus Santa Clara, Santa Cruz, San Benito, and Monterey counties.

C. — — — — — ☐2 — — — —

Mendocino (California's northernmost wine county) and famous Sonoma county are here. Napa and Lake counties aren't on the Pacific coast, but they're still included in this region.

D. — ☐6 — — — — ☐12 — — — — — — —

A rebirth of winemaking sprouts in this territory. It contains fabled El Dorado, Amador, Calaveras, and Tuolomne counties.

E. — — — — — —☐11 — — — — ☐9 — — — —

San Luis Obispo and Santa Barbara counties here were planted extensively in the 1970's and 1980's. Includes the growing Paso Robles district.

F. — — — ☐1 — — — — — — ☐5 — —

This hotter region grows 80% of the state's wine grapes. Parts of Yolo, San Joaquin, Sacramento, Stanislaus, Merced, Madera, Fresno, Tulare, and Kern counties comprise it.

Now, place the boxed letters above onto their matching-numbered spaces below. You'll spell the name of a renowned wine man. For over 45 years a winemaker and consultant in California, Washington, and Oregon, he pioneered new concepts such as the cold fermentation of white wine and the use of small barrels for aging.

André — — — — — — — — — — — — —
             1 2 3 4 5 6 7 8 9 10 11 12 12

36. Noble Napa

The Indian name Napa means "plenty." Napa County and its famous Napa Valley grow plenty of wineries – around 200. Travel along with us. On the facing page, we described **7 wine districts** in Napa County (**A–G**). Next to each **District Description** is a **Picture Clue.** Our **7 Picture Clues**, together with our map, will help you to **identify each district and write its name** onto the blanks. When you finish, do the **Final Answer (H)** and discover one more prime Napa district.

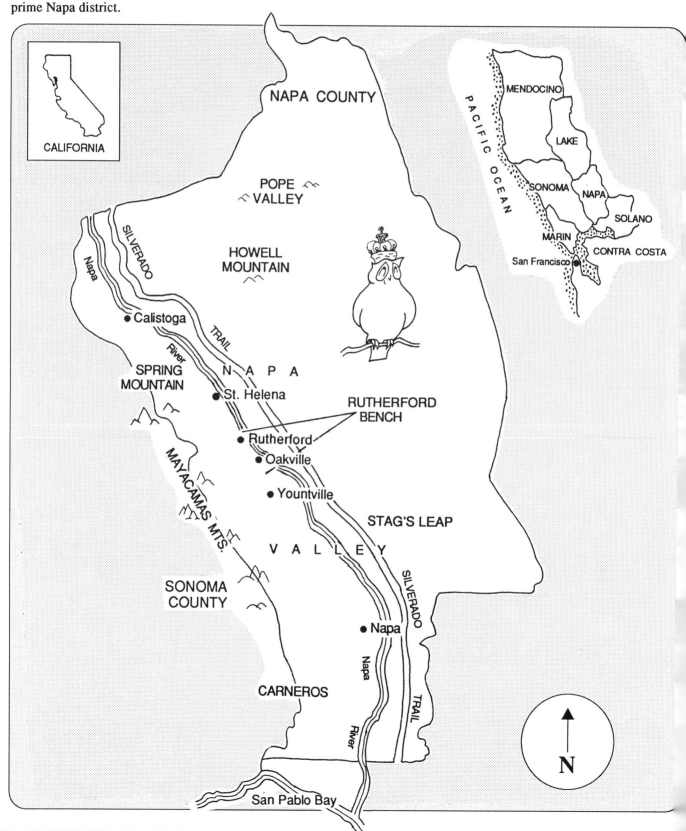

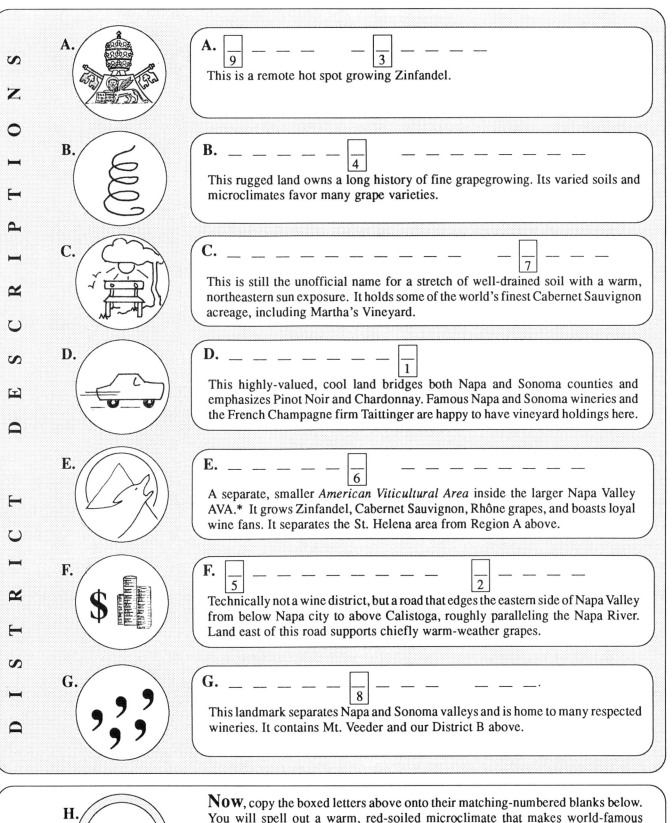

DISTRICT DESCRIPTIONS

A.

A. [9] _ _ _   _ [3] _ _ _

This is a remote hot spot growing Zinfandel.

B.

B. _ _ _ _ _ [4] _ _ _ _ _ _ _

This rugged land owns a long history of fine grapegrowing. Its varied soils and microclimates favor many grape varieties.

C.

C. _ _ _ _ _ _ _ _ _ _ [7] _ _ _

This is still the unofficial name for a stretch of well-drained soil with a warm, northeastern sun exposure. It holds some of the world's finest Cabernet Sauvignon acreage, including Martha's Vineyard.

D.

D. _ _ _ _ _ _ _ [1]

This highly-valued, cool land bridges both Napa and Sonoma counties and emphasizes Pinot Noir and Chardonnay. Famous Napa and Sonoma wineries and the French Champagne firm Taittinger are happy to have vineyard holdings here.

E.

E. _ _ _ _ _ [6] _ _ _ _ _ _

A separate, smaller *American Viticultural Area* inside the larger Napa Valley AVA.* It grows Zinfandel, Cabernet Sauvignon, Rhône grapes, and boasts loyal wine fans. It separates the St. Helena area from Region A above.

F.

F. [5] _ _ _ _ _ _ _ _ [2] _ _ _ _

Technically not a wine district, but a road that edges the eastern side of Napa Valley from below Napa city to above Calistoga, roughly paralleling the Napa River. Land east of this road supports chiefly warm-weather grapes.

G.

G. _ _ _ _ _ [8] _ _ _   _ _ _.

This landmark separates Napa and Sonoma valleys and is home to many respected wineries. It contains Mt. Veeder and our District B above.

H.

Now, copy the boxed letters above onto their matching-numbered blanks below. You will spell out a warm, red-soiled microclimate that makes world-famous Cabernet Sauvignon wines.

H. $\frac{\quad}{1}\frac{\quad}{2}\frac{\quad}{3}\frac{\quad}{4}\frac{\quad}{5},\ \frac{\quad}{6}\frac{\quad}{7}\frac{\quad}{8}\frac{\quad}{9}$

American Viticultural Areas are defined and approved by the federal government, so that bottle labels can clearly state a wine's specific origin. AVA's don't indicate quality control.

37. Napa Notables

Small Napa County is crammed with some 200 wineries. We packed 60 of them into the wordfind on the facing page – see if you can find them all. Our wordfind design is based on the Rhine House of Beringer/Los Hermanos Vineyards in St. Helena. Built in the late 1800's by Jacob and Frederick Beringer, who were German immigrant winemakers, it also boasts thousands of feet of limestone caves visited by tourists.

NAPA WINERIES

Just the bold, **CAPITALIZED** words are in the wordfind.

ACACIA W., Napa
BEAULIEU Vd., Rutherford
BERINGER Vds./Los Hermanos Vds., St. Helena
BOUCHAINE Vds., Napa
BURGESS Cs., St. Helena
CAIN Cs., St. Helena
CAKEBREAD Cs., Rutherford
CARNEROS Creek W., Napa
CAYMUS Vds., Rutherford
CHAPPELLET W., St. Helena
Chateau **CHEVALIER** W., St. Helena
Chateau **MONTELENA** W., Calistoga
CLOS DU VAL Wine Co., Napa
CLOS PEGASE, Calistoga
CUVAISON, Calistoga
DOMAINE CHANDON, Yountville
DUCKHORN Vds., St. Helena
FAR NIENTE W., Oakville
FOLIE À DEUX, St. Helena
FORMAN Vds., St. Helena
FRANCISCAN Vds., Rutherford
FREEMARK Abbey W., St. Helena
GRGICH Hills C., Rutherford
HEITZ Wine Cs., St. Helena
HESS Collection W., Napa
INGLENOOK Napa Valley, Rutherford
HANNS KORNELL Champagne Cs., St. Helena
CHARLES KRUG W., St. Helena
LONG Vds., St. Helena
MARKHAM W., St. Helena

Louis M. **MARTINI**, St. Helena
MAYACAMAS Vds., Napa
MERLION W., St. Helena
Robert **MONDAVI** W., Oakville
Mont **ST. JOHN** Cs., Napa
MONTICELLO Cs., Yountville
Niebaum-**COPPOLA** Estate, Rutherford
PEJU Province, Rutherford
JOSEPH PHELPS Vds., St. Helena
PINE RIDGE W., Napa
QUAIL RIDGE Cs. & Vds., Napa
RAYMOND Vd. and C., St. Helena
ROUND HILL W., St. Helena
RUTHERFORD HILL W., Rutherford
SCHRAMSBERG Vds., Calistoga
SCHUG Cs., Napa
Charles F. **SHAW** Vd. & W., St. Helena
SILVER OAK Wine Cs., Oakville
SILVERADO Vds., Napa
SMITH-MADRONE Vds., St. Helena
SPRING MOUNTAIN Vds., St. Helena
STAG'S LEAP Wine Cs., Napa
STERLING Vds., Calistoga
STONY HILL Vd., St. Helena
SUTTER HOME W., St. Helena
TREFETHEN Vds., Napa
VICHON W., Oakville
Villa **MT. EDEN** W., Oakville
WILLIAM HILL W., Napa
WHITE ROCK Vds., Napa

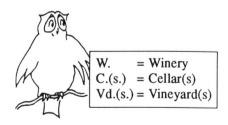

W.	= Winery
C.(s.)	= Cellar(s)
Vd.(s.)	= Vineyard(s)

DAFFY DEFINITION: NAPA – A northern Californian word meaning *"brief siesta."*

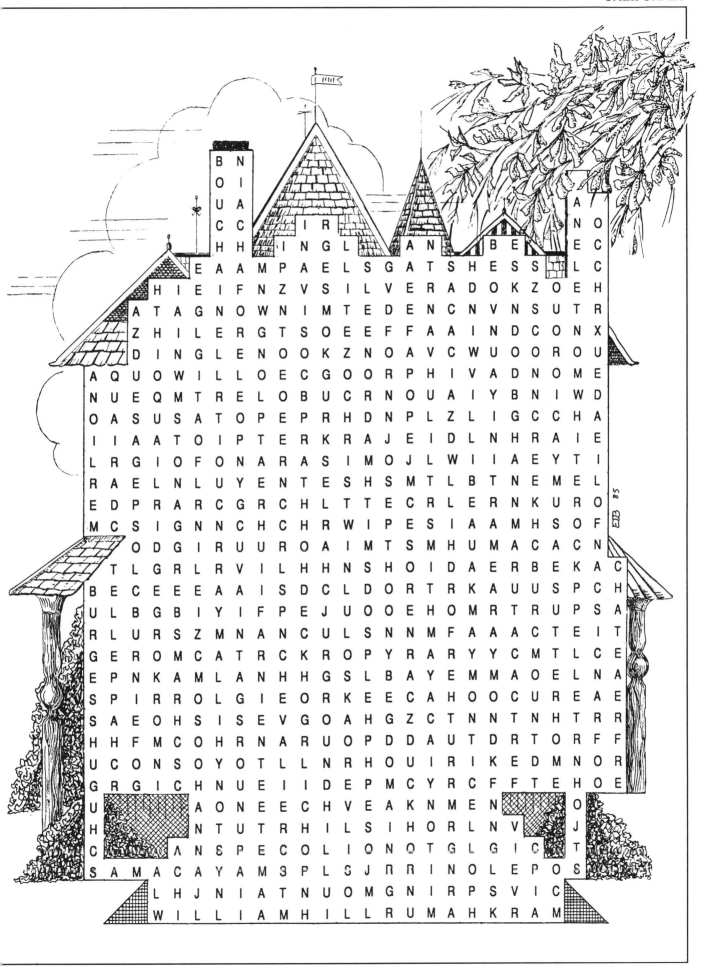

38. Sonoma Survey

Napa's high acreage prices kindled renewed growth in neighboring, historic Sonoma county. Today, Sonoma county is revitalized: its distinct viticultural zones, ranging from cool in the south towards warmer in the north, create welcomed and acclaimed wines. Explore this unique, wonderful county with us. You'll have to match up our **6 Sonoma Wine Areas (A – F)** with our **6 Sonoma Wine Area Descriptions (1 – 6).** How? We drew Sonoma's beautiful Jordan Vineyard and Winery (located near Healdsburg) in 6 stages, adding details as we progressed. Each drawing has a Sonoma Wine Area name attached to it. **Put the 6 drawings in proper sequence.** When you do, the Wine Area Name attached to the first drawing will match Wine Area Description #1; the Wine Area Name attached to the second drawing will match Wine Area Description #2, and so on.

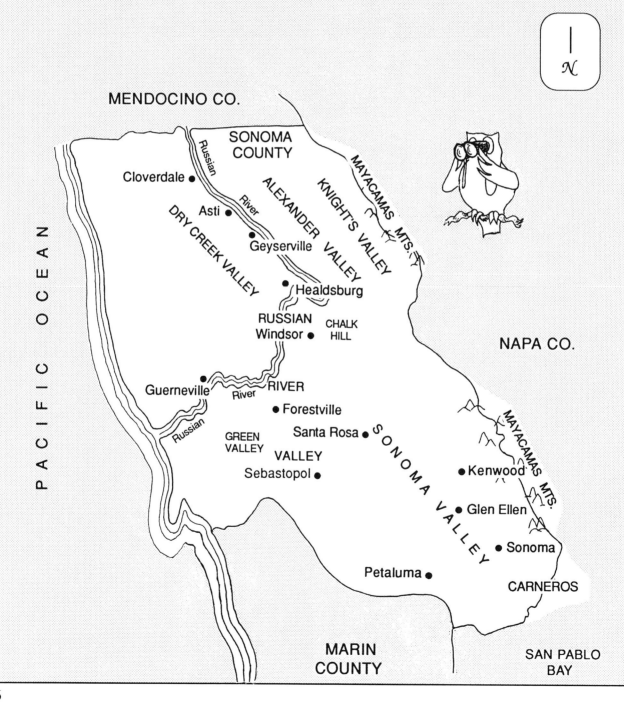

A. ____ Carneros

Jordan Vineyard and
Winery, Healdsburg

B. ____ Knight's Valley

Jordan Vineyard and
Winery, Healdsburg

C. ____ Dry Creek

Jordan Vineyard and
Winery, Healdsburg

D. ____ Russian River Valley

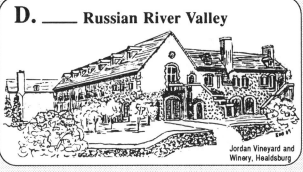

Jordan Vineyard and
Winery, Healdsburg

E. ____ Sonoma Valley

Jordan Vineyard and
Winery, Healdsburg

F. ____ Alexander Valley

Jordan Vineyard and
Winery, Healdsburg

Wine Area Descriptions

1. Although Cabernet Sauvignon and Zinfandel grow in its warmer spots, this cool zone specializes in Pinot Noir and Chardonnay: it supplies those grapes to sparkling winemakers here and elsewhere. Enclosed within this large viticultural area is Green Valley, a cool district fine for the sparkling wine grapes, Pinot Noir and Chardonnay. Also included is part of the Chalk Hill zone, named for its white volcanic earth, where white grapes – especially Chardonnay and Sauvignon Blanc – predominate.

2. Also known as The Valley Of The Moon, this district includes Area #3 and is itself famous for Chardonnay, Zinfandel, and Cabernet Sauvignon.

3. A cool area valued and shared by Napa and Sonoma counties, it's the home of famous Winery Lake Vineyard.

4. Home of prized vineyards *(Alexander's Crown, Robert Young, Marlstone)*, this warm land (with some cool spots) grows Chardonnay, Cabernet Sauvignon, Merlot, Gewürztraminer, Johannisberg Riesling, and Zinfandel.

5. This area's old vines make deep Zinfandels. It grows Cabernet Sauvignon and Sauvignon Blanc in its warmer sections, and Pinot Noir and Chardonnay in the cooler ones.

6. A small, warmer tract that grows Cabernet Sauvignon and Sauvignon Blanc.

39. Sonoma Specialists

Circle 43 well-known Sonoma county wineries. They're going in all different directions inside the mission on the facing page. The mission is Sonoma city's Mission San Francisco Solano de Sonoma, the last in the California mission chain begun by Father Junípero Serra. Founded July 4, 1923 by Father José Altamira, it's now preserved and part of California's park system. The large Sonoma County wine festival starts the last week of September and includes the traditional blessing of the grapes on the Mission grounds.

SONOMA WINERIES

Just the bold, **CAPITALIZED** words below are in the wordfind.

ALEXANDER VALLEY Vds., Healdsburg
BUENA VISTA W. Carneros Estate, Sonoma
Davis **BYNUM** W., Healdsburg
Chateau **DE BAUN**, Santa Rosa
Chateau **ST. JEAN**, Kenwood
Chateau **SOUVERAIN**, Geyserville
CLOS DU BOIS, Healdsburg
DE LOACH Vds., Santa Rosa
Domaine **LAURIER** W. & Vds., Forestville
Domaine **ST. GEORGE** W., Healdsburg
DRY CREEK Vd., Healdsburg
FERRARI-Carano W., Healdsburg
FIELD STONE W. & Vd., Healdsburg
FOPPIANO Vds., Healdsburg
GEYSER PEAK W., Geyserville
GLEN ELLEN Vds. & W., Glen Ellen
GLORIA Ferrer (Freixenet), Sonoma
GRAND CRU Vds., Glen Ellen
GUNDLACH–BUNDSCHU W., Vineburg
HACIENDA Wine Cs., Sonoma
HANZELL Vds., Sonoma
HOP KILN W., Griffin Vd., Healdsburg

IRON HORSE Vds., Sebastopol
JORDAN Vd. & W., Healdsburg
KENWOOD Vds., Kenwood
F. **KORBEL** & Bros., Guerneville
La **CREMA**, Petaluma
LAMBERT BRIDGE, Healdsburg
LYTTON SPRINGS W., Healdsburg
MARK WEST Vds., Forestville
MATANZAS CREEK W., Santa Rosa
MERRY VINTNERS, Santa Rosa
MILL Creek Vds., Healdsburg
Pat **PAULSEN** Vds., Cloverdale
J. **PEDRONCELLI** W., Geyserville
PIPER SONOMA Cs., Windsor
PRESTON Vds., Healdsburg
SAUSAL W., Healdsburg
SEBASTIANI Vds., Sonoma
SIMI W., Healdsburg
SMOTHERS Bros. Wines, Kenwood
Rodney **STRONG** Vds., Windsor
VIANSA W., Sonoma

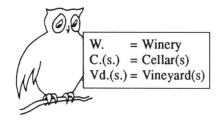

W.	= Winery
C.(s.)	= Cellar(s)
Vd.(s.)	= Vineyard(s)

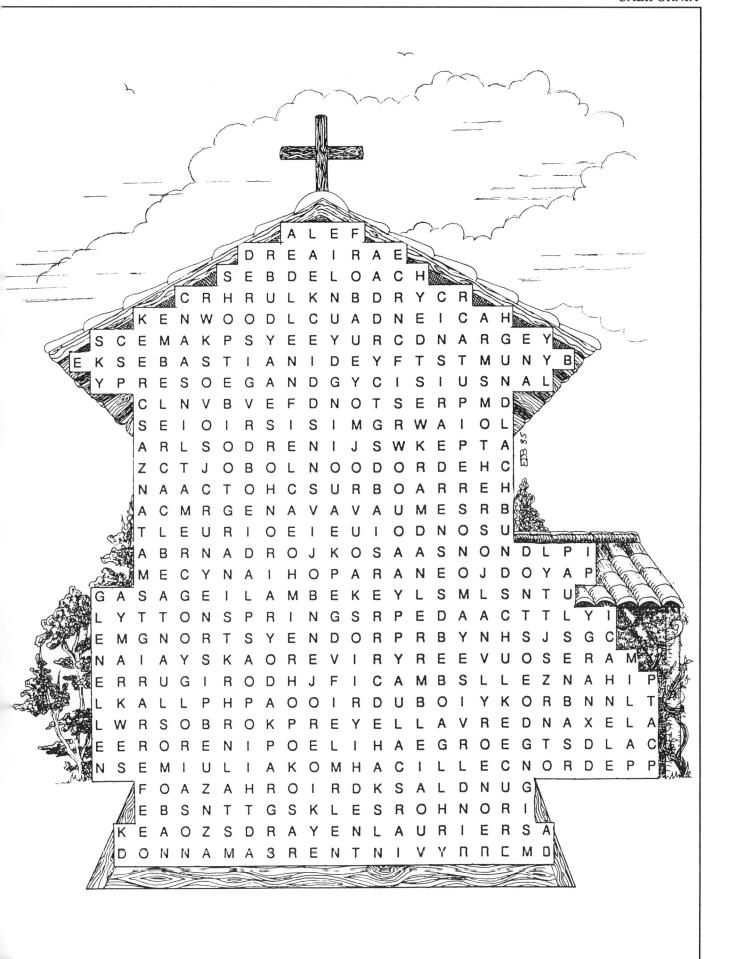

A L E F
D R E A I R A E
S E B D E L O A C H
C R H R U L K N B D R Y C R
K E N W O O D L C U A D N E I C A H
S C E M A K P S Y E E Y U R C D N A R G E Y
E K S E B A S T I A N I D E Y F T S T M U N Y B
Y P R E S O E G A N D G Y C I S I U S N A L
C L N V B V E F D N O T S E R P M D
S E I O I R S I S I M G R W A I O L
A R L S O D R E N I J S W K E P T A
Z C T J O B O L N O O D O R D E H C
N A A C T O H C S U R B O A R R E H
A C M R G E N A V A V A U M E S R B
T L E U R I O E I E U I O D N O S U
A B R N A D R O J K O S A A S N O N D L P I
M E C Y N A I H O P A R A N E O J D O Y A P
G A S A G E I L A M B E K E Y L S M L S N T U
L Y T T O N S P R I N G S R P E D A A C T T L Y I
E M G N O R T S Y E N D O R P R B Y N H S J S G C
N A I A Y S K A O R E V I R Y R E E V U O S E R A M
E R R U G I R O D H J F I C A M B S L L E Z N A H I P
L K A L L P H P A O O I R D U B O I Y K O R B N N L T
L W R S O B R O K P R E Y E L L A V R E D N A X E L A
E E R O R E N I P O E L I H A E G R O E G T S D L A C
N S E M I U L I A K O M H A C I L L E C N O R D E P P
F O A Z A H R O I R D K S A L D N U G
E B S N T T G S K L E S R O H N O R I
K E A O Z S D R A Y E N L A U R I E R S A
D O N N A M A 3 R E N T N I V Y Π Γ C M D

40. Mendocino And Lake Counties

Fill the blanks and meet California's northernmost wine counties. Each of our California poppy's petals and leaves needs an "E" added to its letters to make words. Each completed word fits into the blank with its matching number.

Mendocino County is the (1_____ home of proud, independent grape farmers and the site of several major growing regions. Most of these regions have warm climates.

Near the coast, *Anderson Valley* is Mendocino's (2_____ area: it specializes in Pinot Noir, Chardonnay, Riesling, and Gewürztraminer. Its noted wineries are: Navarro, Husch, Roederer (the French Champagne firm), and Scharffenberger Cellars, a sparkling wine facility now owned chiefly by the French Champagne firm, Pommery. Kendall-Jackson (in Lake Co.) bought and replanted Edmeades Vineyard with the sparkling wine grapes Chardonnay and Pinot Noir.

Twelve miles long, the *Ukiah Valley* boasts the largest Mendocino county grape (3_____. It emphasizes Zinfandel, Chardonnay, Riesling, and Cabernet Sauvignon. Parson's Creek Winery and the respected Parducci Winery are in *Ukiah Valley*.

South of *Ukiah Valley*, solar-powered McDowell Valley Vineyards applied for and (4_____ a one-winery American Viticultural Area designation, *McDowell Valley*. It produces Chardonnay, Cabernet Sauvignon, and Rhône varieties. Northeast of Ukiah, *Potter Valley* grows (5_____, Chardonnay and Pinot Noir. Nearby *Redwood Valley*'s (6_____ climate promotes several varieties, including Zinfandel, Cabernet Sauvignon, Chardonnay, and Sauvignon Blanc. *Redwood Valley* is home to the formidable Fetzer family enterprise and Weibel moved its entire sparkling wine operation to there from Livermore.

Lightly (7_____ Lake County plants Cabernet Sauvignon, is praised for its Sauvignon Blancs, and also grows Zinfandel, Chardonnay, Chenin Blanc, and Merlot. Most grapes flourish at the south end of Clear Lake and in *Guenoc Valley*. Wineries of note are: modern Guenoc Winery (the former home of Lillie Langtry, the famous British Victorian actress, and the only winery in the *Guenoc Valley* American Viticultural Area), Kendall-Jackson Vineyards, and Konocti Winery. Several wineries in Mendocino, Sonoma, and Napa counties own extensive grape acreage here.

Vertical left margin: LAKE / MENDOCINO

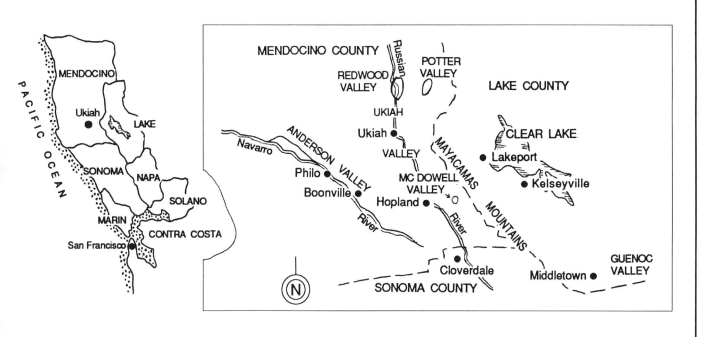

41. Central Coast – Bay Area

CALIFORNIA

Urbanization squeezed the Bay Area to a fraction of its former winegrowing size. Alameda County is the star player here, with celebrated Livermore Valley and white varieties: Sauvignon Blanc, Chardonnay, Sémillon, and Grey Riesling. It is the home of respected Concannon Vineyards and of the illustrious pioneering Wente Bros. family business. Weibel moved to Mendocino County.

Read one last sentence about this locality by putting these words in order.

Mystery Sentence

vineyards is remaining noticeable here, more sprawl but

some Urban protects than new acreage. zoning

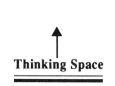

Thinking Space

42. Central Coast

We've looked at the northern tip of the Central Coast in the previous puzzle (Puzzle #41 – Bay Area, p. 61). Let's see the rest of this domain. Read our sentences below: the **underlined** wineries there cleverly arranged themselves in our wordfind on the facing page. Find them! (Only when you're ready – don't let us push you into anything.)

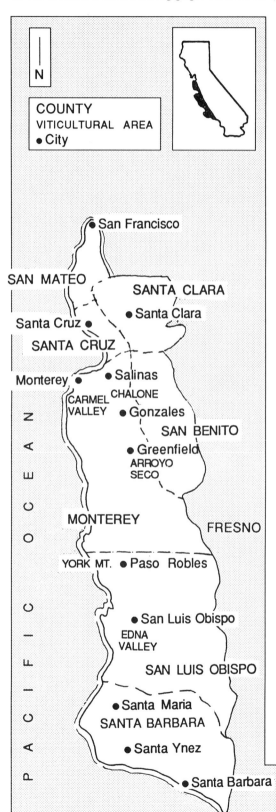

SANTA CLARA County. Urbanization reduced this county's massive grape acreage. Most wineries import grapes from other counties. Some well-known wineries: **Mount Eden**, **Ridge**, San Martin, Kathryn Kennedy, Congress Springs, J. Lohr, and the eminent family **Mirassou**.

SANTA CRUZ County. There are few vineyards here – many grapes are imported from other counties. The *Santa Cruz Mountain* appellation follows the border between Santa Cruz and Santa Clara counties, and includes a part of San Mateo County. It's a region of active maverick experimentation with many varieties and styles, including those from the French Rhône country. Some prize-winning wineries: **Ahlgren**, **Bonny Doon**, David Bruce, **Roudon-Smith**, and Santa Cruz Mountain.

MONTEREY County. The situation here is reversed from Santa Cruz – here there are few wineries and over 30,000 acres planted to grapes. The chief growing area is in *Salinas Valley*. Ocean breezes run down from the Bay to give a long, cool growing season. White grapes rule – Chardonnay, Chenin Blanc, Johannisberg Riesling, Sauvignon Blanc, Pinot Blanc, Gewürztraminer, and red Cabernet Sauvignon and Zinfandel. American Viticultural Areas (AVAs) are *Arroyo Seco*, *Carmel Valley*, and *Chalone*. Some noted wineries: Château Julien, **Jekel**, Smith & Hook, **Chalone**, **Ventana**.

SAN LUIS OBISPO County. The undulating hills here cradle 2 major winegrowing sites. Warm *Paso Robles* in the north receives no sea air. Its grapes: Zinfandel, Sauvignon Blanc, Chardonnay, Chenin Blanc, and Syrah. Cool *Edna Valley* to the south is freshened by fog and ocean influences. It raises Chardonnay, Pinot Noir, and Sauvignon Blanc. Some of the county's wineries: Arciero, Corbett Canyon, **Creston** Vineyards, **Eberle**, **Edna Valley**, **Justin**, **Meridian**, **Maison Deutz**, **Martin Bros.**, Wild Horse, and Mastantuono.

SANTA BARBARA County also harbors 2 major grapegrowing provinces. Cool *Santa Maria Valley* is a popular source of Chardonnay grapes, plus Pinot Noir, Johannisberg Riesling, Sauvignon Blanc, Gewürztraminer, Cabernet Sauvignon and Merlot. *Santa Ynez Valley* has been narrowing in on Chardonnay, Johannisberg Riesling, and Pinot Noir. Some wineries: Brander, **Byron**, **Firestone**, Gainey, **Qupé**, **Sanford**, Santa Ynez Winery, **Mosby**, **Zaca Mesa**, Sterns Wharf.

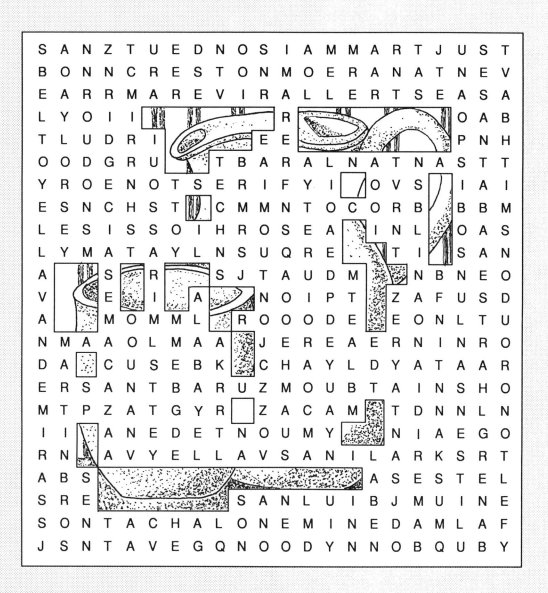

S A N Z T U E D N O S I A M M A R T J U S T
B O N N C R E S T O N M O E R A N A T N E V
E A R R M A R E V I R A L L E R T S E A S A
L Y O I I   R   O A B
T L U D R I   E E   P N H
O O D G R U   T B A R A L N A T N A S T T
Y R O E N O T S E R I F Y I   O V S   I A I
E S N C H S T   C M M N T O C O R B   B B M
L E S I S S O I H R O S E A   I N L   O A S
L Y M A T A Y L N S U Q R E   T I   S A N
A   S   R   S J T A U D M   N B N E O
V   E   I A   N O I P T   Z A F U S D
A   M O M M L   R O O O D E   E O N L T U
N M A A O L M A A   J E R E A E R N I N R O
D A   C U S E B K   C H A Y L D Y A T A A R
E R S A N T B A R U Z M O U B T A I N S H O
M T P Z A T G Y R   Z A C A M   T D N N L N
I I   A N E D E T N O U M Y   N I A E G O
R N   A V Y E L L A V S A N I L A R K S R T
A B S   A S E S T E L
S R E   S A N L U I B J M U I N E
S O N T A C H A L O N E M I N E D A M L A F
J S N T A V E G Q N O O D Y N N O B Q U B Y

Our grid is based on the open containers and water pitchers that are a necessary part of every wine tasting. If you don't like the wine, or you don't care to drink too much, empty your glass into the container, swish it around with water, and empty it once again. This also prepares the glass for the next wine.

43. Central Valley

Are you familiar with logic puzzles? We give you clues and you must reason your way to the answers. Try this logic game and, at the same time, visit California's vast grape cornucopia. Almost 80% of all California wine grapes come from this hot, fertile realm. This is also the home of the largest wineries in California. Ready?

	Geography	Grapes	Wineries	Wine progress	Book	Article	Phone Call	Interview
STEVE								
ANN								
ADONI								
FELICIA								
Book		O						
Article		O						
Phone Call	O	+	O	O				
Interview		O						

Four students at an agricultural college received their assignment – investigate the southern Central Valley wine scene. **See if you can deduce which student gathered what information and from where.** Here's a start: we marked on the grid the data that we discovered from Clue #5 below. Continue on and solve our query.

Here's the information that our students found:

Geography: This southern portion of the Central Valley is also called San Joaquin Valley. It runs approximately 300 miles south through San Joaquin, Stanislaus, Madera, Fresno, Tulare, and Kern counties between the Sierra Nevada and the Coast Range mountains. Wine activity centers in Modesto, Fresno, and Bakersfield cities.

Grapes: Hot weather grapes thrive in here: Barbera, Carignane, Carnelian, Chenin Blanc, Grenache, Ruby Cabernet, French Colombard, Zinfandel, plus 200,000 acres of Thompson Seedless. Although it's considered an eating, not a wine, grape, Thompson Seedless forms the bulk of many low-end, generic California blended and sparkling wines.

Wineries: Some VBWs (Very Big Wineries) are headed by E & J Gallo, the world's largest winemaker. (It sells 1 out of every 3 bottles of wine in the U.S.) Large winery facilities are also owned by Franzia (The Wine Group), Delicato, Royal Host, and the growers' co-ops, Guild and Gibson.

Wine Progress: At one time, table wines from the south Central valley were flawed, flat, cooked, and over-sweetened. It's still known as the largest producer of jug, fortified, and distilled wines, but now the south Central Valley uses cold fermentation and scientific cultivation to make flavorful, crisp table wines. Some wineries – Papagni Vineyards in Madera, for example – prove that the Central Valley can produce fine, high quality wines.

CLUES:

1. Each student uncovered one kind of information. One student found **geographic data**; another studied Central Valley **grapes**; a third surveyed the area's **wineries**; the fourth got an idea of the region's overall **wine progress**.

2. Each student found information from a different source: **a book** on California; **a magazine article**; a **phone call** to a friend in Modesto; and an **interview** with a wine store owner in his shop.

3. Felicia and Ann talked to no one; Steve stayed home.

4. The wine store owner mentioned the area's use of modern technology.

5. The phone call gave one student the grape information.

6. Ann used the library, but she found no geographical data.

7. The book was borrowed during a visit to an uncle's private collection.

44. Central Valley – Something Else

Unscramble our **bold, mixed-up words** for facts about Central Valley port wines – delicious brandy-fortified treats.

For **nasteegroni**, the Ficklin **maylif** of Madera has **dalpten neeginu** Portuguese grapes and **deniofsah** them into **dreepsect** port **sniwe**.

The **wreen** port **rekam** in the area, Quady, also **setreca alpurpo streeds** wines from Muscat **persag**.

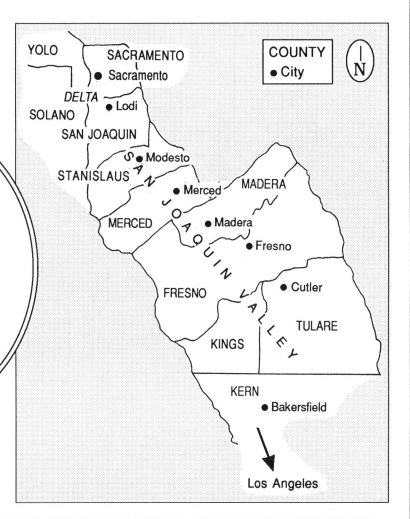

COUNTY
● City

YOLO
SACRAMENTO
● Sacramento
DELTA
SOLANO
● Lodi
SAN JOAQUIN
● Modesto
STANISLAUS
SAN JOAQUIN VALLEY
● Merced
MADERA
MERCED
● Madera
● Fresno
FRESNO
● Cutler
TULARE
KINGS
KERN
● Bakersfield

Los Angeles

45. Central Valley – Sacramento River Delta

The north arm of the Central Valley reaches up into Sacramento, Yolo, and Solano counties where the Sacramento and San Joaquin rivers form into an unusual growing zone. The Sacramento River Delta, also known as "the Everglades of the West," is filled with waterways and...

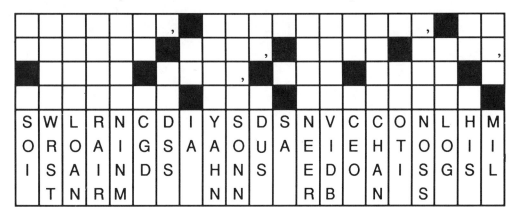

Main Growing Sites: Clarksburg, Merritt Island, Mandeville Island
Main Grapes: .... Chenin Blanc, White Riesling, Cabernet Sauvignon, Merlot, Petite Sirah
Some Wineries:........ Bogle, R & J Cook, Renaissance, Gibson (growers' coop), Winters

(Directions are with Puzzle #14, pg. 24.)

46. Sierra Foothills

Ready to play? Our story below has **35 underlined** words. Nine of those **underlined** words (**we're not saying** *which* **nine**) are in the wordfind below: **the 26 remaining underlined words fit onto the grid.**

   Let's hike around the **dry**, golden-hilled **Sierra Nevada*** territory. Grape growing **here** started in **Gold Rush*** days: after decades of neglect, it's again on an **upswing**. The most winery-populated counties are El Dorado, Amador, and Calaveras. A conversation with Scott **Harvey**, winemaker of praised **Santino** Wines at **Plymouth**, produced most of **our** Sierra Foothills information below.

   This **warm**, dry-farmed, **historic** region receives rain only in **winter** or early spring. **Hot** Sacramento Valley air and Delta breezes rule the days here, while **mountain** air creeps down to **chill** the nights. Zinfandel is the grape most folks **associate** with this region, and other Californian wineries (most notably, Napa's Sutter Home) rely on Foothills **Zinfandel** grapes. However, a myriad of other varieties flourish here, including French Rhône Syrah **and** Mourvèdre, Italian **Nebbiolo** and Sangiovese, and Portuguese Tinta port grapes.

   Scott and other **Amador** County vintners created a judging **panel** that evaluates each participating winery's **new** wines. This panel grants a special Amador County **quality** approval to wines that **pass** its **evaluation**. Quality judgments like this are foreign to **the** U.S.'s freewheeling marketing mentality, but such **European**-style **approval** panels could be California's marketing wave of the future.

   Some Sierra Foothills wineries: Amador Foothill, **Boeger**, **Sobon** Estate, **Karly**, Kenworthy, **Monteviña**, Santino, **Shenandoah**, **Stevenot**, Story, Winterbrook.

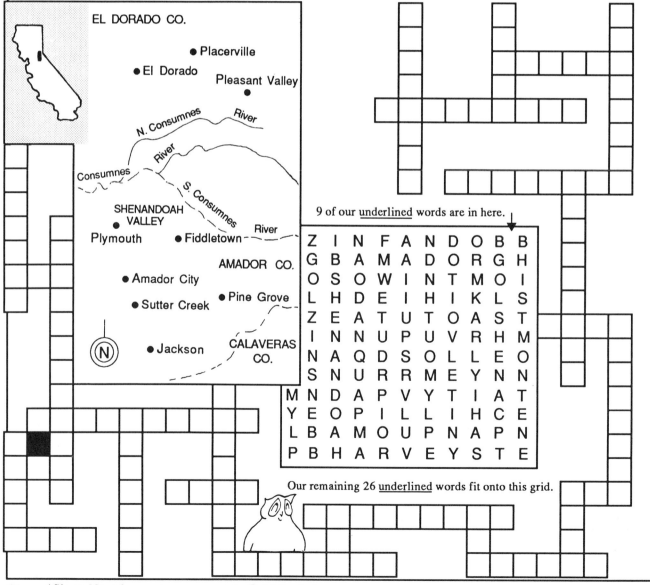

9 of our underlined words are in here.

Z	I	N	F	A	N	D	O	B	B
G	B	A	M	A	D	O	R	G	H
O	S	O	W	I	N	T	M	O	I
L	H	D	E	I	H	I	K	L	S
Z	E	A	T	U	T	O	A	S	T
I	N	N	U	P	U	V	R	H	M
N	A	Q	D	S	O	L	L	E	O
S	N	U	R	R	M	E	Y	N	N
M	N	D	A	P	V	Y	T	I	A	T
Y	E	O	P	I	L	L	I	H	C	E
L	B	A	M	O	U	P	N	A	P	N
P	B	H	A	R	V	E	Y	S	T	E

Our remaining 26 underlined words fit onto this grid.

47. South Coast

California's first vines were planted in its southern section. Today, some South Coast areas are growing, while other South Coast districts display more history than they do growth. Read on, then enjoy yourself by putting our 31 **underlined** words and wineries into their correct spaces below.

In San Bernardino County, **urbanization** gobbled up the famous **hot Cucamonga** vineyards. Local wineries make everyday wines from old **Mission grape** vines or from Central Valley grapes. In Los Angeles, wineries market their uniqueness as wineries in the Big City.

On the other hand, **Riverside** County is **increasing** its acreage of **cool** and medium-warm weather grapes, especially around Temecula, a fast-developing region. "Temecula" is a California **Indian** term for "*where the sun shines through the white mist*." Twenty-five miles from the ocean, Temecula receives cooling air through the Santa Margarita Gap, but rare **rainfall**. During the 1980's, these sleepy hills woke up to new roads, new housing and business complexes, and new **wineries**. Callaway, a leading winery, chose to create only **white wines**, since white grapes, notably **Sauvignon Blanc***, Riesling, Chenin Blanc, Chardonnay, and Muscat Canelli, produce **well** here. Red grape **experimentation** continues, especially with Cabernet Sauvignon, Petite Sirah, **Merlot**, and with some Italian varieties such as **Sangiovese** and **Barbera**.

Some South Coast wineries: **Los Angeles**: Donatoni, Palos Verdes, San Antonio. **Ventura** Co.: **Daumé**, **Leeward**, Rolling Hills. **Temecula**: Baily, **Callaway**, Maurice Carrie, Cilurzo, **Clos Du Muriel**, **Culbertson**, Filsinger, French Valley, **Hart**, Mount Palomar, Piconi. **San Diego** Co.: Bernardo, Ferrara, Menghini.

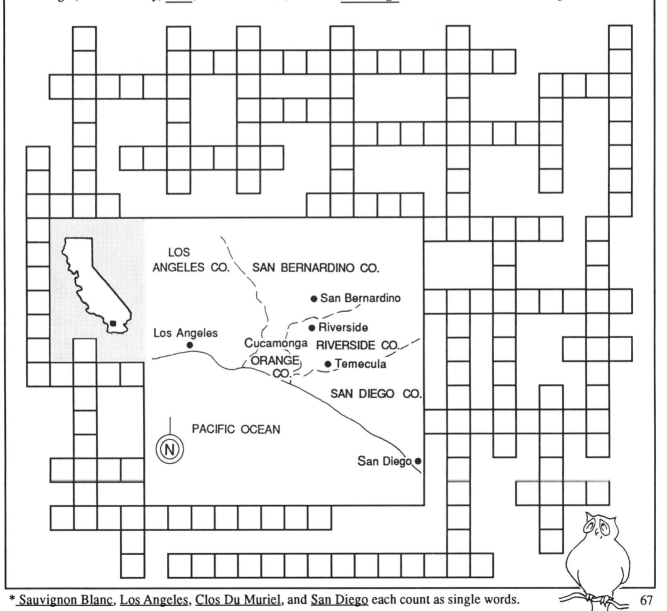

---

* <u>Sauvignon Blanc</u>, <u>Los Angeles</u>, <u>Clos Du Muriel</u>, and <u>San Diego</u> each count as single words.

California Wine Trends

Like the uncertain strata beneath it, California's wine scene constantly shifts, adjusts, and shifts again. Our ace reporter, Devon Trueblood, has uncovered highlights of this changing panorama. To keep his scoops secret until we go to press, Devon disguised his reports (Puzzles #48 through #53). Start detecting!

48. Trend – Situation Changing

California's big advantage is its openness to new winemaking methods.

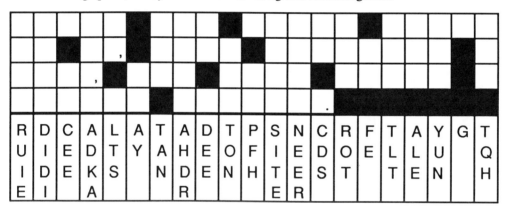

With amazing speed, many innovative marketing and technological...

R	D		C	A	L	A		A	D	T	P	S	N		C	R	F		T	A	Y	G		T
U	I		E	D	T	Y	T	H	E	O	F	I	E		D	O	E		L	L	U			Q
I	D		E	K	S		A	D	E	N	H	T	E		S	T			T	E	N			H
E	I			A			N	R				E	R											

Puzzle directions are with Puzzle #17, p. 24.

49. Trend – Varietals

Varietal wines aren't what they used to be. See what's new by unscrambling the **BOLD** words below.

CYKUL vineyards can **TOBAS** a **ENQUIU** soil type, hill exposure, or microclimate that produces grapes very **FREDTINEF** from those of **RETOH** vineyards. More and more **KRENMAWSEI** select a **OREFTAVI** vineyard and **KEMA MESO** varietal wines solely from its **CINVIDTIETS** grapes. Chateau St. Jean's *Robert Young Vineyards* Chardonnay is one delicious **PEMXALE**.

A continuing trend in varietal wines is the **VEMO YAAW** from aggressive **REPWO** and towards softer, more **TEBLUS** flavors.

50. Trend – Blend

Winemaking's taking a turn away from 100% varietals. Blend the right words below and see what we mean. Follow our directions carefully, cross out the unnecessary words, and read each line **across** for the blending story.

A. In Column A, cross out all plural words except those with the word "wine" in them. Cross out all words that mean "to communicate."

B. In Column B, cross out all abbreviations. Cross out all the words that contain one or more of the letters **j**, **k**, **x**, **y**, or **z**.

C. In Column C, cross out all words with more than 9 letters, unless they start with "C," and all words with less than 4 letters, unless they end with "**X**."

D. In Column D, cross out foreign words except French ones. Cross out all two-word combinations.

E. In Column E, cross out words with a footnote attached, unless they start with C, L, M, or N. Cross out all contractions, if they're negative.

F. In Column F, keep all two-word combinations. Cross out single words that start with a letter that precedes "**S**" in the alphabet or that follows "**W**" in the alphabet.

A	B	C	D	E	F
MANY	PRIZED	BLENDED	WINES	CAN'T	STILL USE
ORDINARY	GRAPES,	ANY	THAT SEE	PROVISION [1]	FOR EXAMPLE
VARIETALS.	THE	THOMPSON	SEEDLESS,	AS	THEIR BASE.
HOWEVER,	THE	MODERNIZED	NEW	TREND	CONTINUES
PHENOMENA	IS TO BLEND	THE	SEVERAL	NOBLE	VARIETIES
TOGETHER	ESP.	INTO	*VINO*	PREMIUM	WINES. FOR
INSTANCE,	NUMEROUS	CALIFORNIA	WINERIES	WOULDN'T	MAKE BLENDS
AS THEY DO	IN	TANTALIZING	BORDEAUX.[1]	THEY'VE	DECIDED
ALUMNAE	GIVEN	THESE	BORDEAUX	ALSO. [2]	STYLES A
COLLECTIVE	MYSTIC	NAME –	SUCH AS	*MERITAGE* .[2]	PROMOTION.
SPEAK	OTHER	SLY	CALIFORNIA	ADJACENT [3]	WINERIES
GROW AND	*"SACK ":*	COMBINE	THE FINE	GRAPES USED	IN THE
OCTOPI	FRENCH	RHÔNE	REGION,	ELIMINATED.[3]	SUCH AS
GRENACHE,	(REJOINING	ITS	MOURVÈDRE,	AND	CHARDONNAY)
SYRAH,	INTO	DELICIOUS	*SAKE*	TABLE	WINES AND
TRANSMIT.	APERITIFS.	IS	*FRIJOLES.*	ALTHOUGH [1]	DELUXE.
BACTERIA	(ZINFANDEL)	PHYLLOXERA	TO	WON'T	CREATE THE
TALK	MOST	INCREDIBLY	PLEASING	AMONG [2]	TASTES,
WINEMAKERS	SENSIBLY	MIX GRAPES	*RETSINA*	AS	XIMÉNES
BLENDS.	JUDGE	THEY LIKE	AND	SHOULDN'T	EVEN BLEND
FINISHED	WINES FROM	DIVERGENTLY	DIFFERENT	COUNTRIES. [3]	YESTERDAY.

[1] *That is, reds from varying combinations of Cabernet Sauvignon, Cabernet Franc, Merlot, Petit Verdot, and Malbec, and whites from different percentages of Sauvignon Blanc, Sémillon, and/or Muscadelle.*
[2] *Rhymes with 'heritage.' You may see these Bordeaux-style wines listed as **Meritage** on menus and in stores.*
[3] *Christian Bros.' **Montage** marries California and French Médoc wines together in one bottle.*

51. Trend – Only The Best

Another important sign of a maturing California wine industry is coded below in this rhebus.

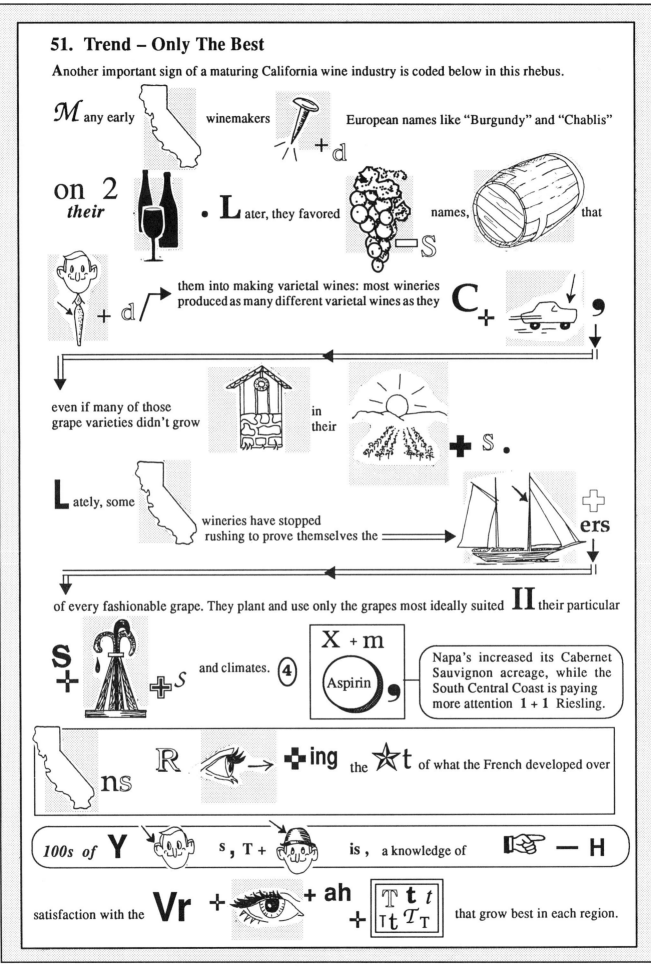

M any early [California] winemakers [nail] + d European names like "Burgundy" and "Chablis"

on 2 *their* [wine] . **L** ater, they favored [grapes] − s [barrel] names, that

[man] + d → them into making varietal wines: most wineries produced as many different varietal wines as they **C** + [car] ;

even if many of those grape varieties didn't grow [house] in their [sunrise over vines] + s .

L ately, some [California] wineries have stopped rushing to prove themselves the ⟶ [schooner] + ers

of every fashionable grape. They plant and use only the grapes most ideally suited **II** their particular

S + [fountain] + s and climates. ④ (X + m / Aspirin) , Napa's increased its Cabernet Sauvignon acreage, while the South Central Coast is paying more attention 1 + 1 Riesling.

[California] ns **R** [eye] → + ing the [star] t of what the French developed over

100s of **Y** [man] s , T + [man with hat] is , a knowledge of [pointing hand] − **H**

satisfaction with the **Vr** + [eye] + ah + [T t t / t T T] that grow best in each region.

52. Trends – Three Other Developments

Our text below has 8 missing words. **Add** the central "I" to each of our 8 groups of scrambled letters. Next, **unscramble** each group and place your completed words on their matching-numbered blanks. Then you can read about 3 notable California wine trends. We used the design below as a reminder that computers guide many modern winery operations, from accounting to monitoring vineyard weather and soil conditions.

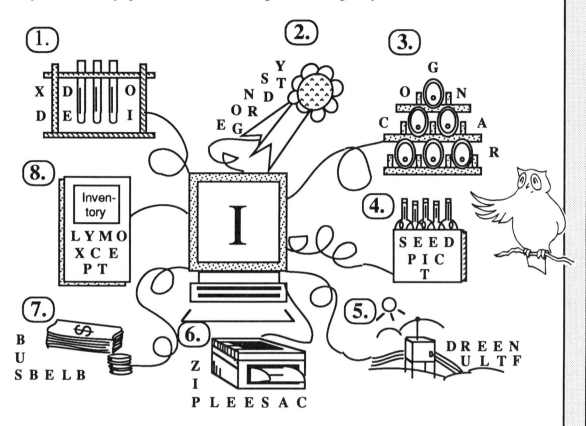

A. Naturally Good. "Natural" winemaking is gaining advocates. Many winemakers, such as Buena Vista's Jill Davis, have already cut their use of sulphur (1_____. Others cut it more by using wild yeasts instead of (2_____ them with SO_2. (3_____ growers, like Mendocino's Frey and Fetzer families and Napa's San Pietro Vara Co., strongly believe in raising (4_____ – free vines and fruit. Tony Coturri makes his wines without fining them or using any added SO_2. Paradise Vintners also shuns any added chemicals. Edna Valley, Glen Ellen, and Meeker wineries are among those who produce some or all (5_____ wines. Napa County is experimenting with a 'self-sustaining' research vineyard. This means a vineyard that uses the least amount of human intervention. The new wine watchword is "bio-wines."

B. Bubbling Over. Over 50 California wineries now produce sparkling wines. Some, such as Korbel, Hanns Kornell, Schramsberg, Culbertson, and Scharffenberger (6_____ in sparklers: others added (7_____ to their regular lists of table wines. Famous French firms – Taittinger, Roederer, Moët & Chandon, and Piper Heidsieck, for examples, desired to expand. They bought California's grape perfect acreage – it sells for much less than comparable land in France.

C. Non-Alcoholic. Consumers are interested in low and non-alcoholic wines. J. Lohr's *Ariel* brand takes out the alcohol by reverse osmosis. It adds a cold fermentation process which is designed to save the wine's (8_____ and flavor.

53. Trend – Here Come The Elephants?

Foreign firms and large U.S. corporations are always looking for profitable investments and political stability, so they've zeroed in on California's wine industry. These companies have built their own new wineries and bought all or part of established ones. Some analysts hold that this means the end of lovingly-crafted, quality masterpieces from maverick innovators: they predict the onset of soul-less, mass-produced liquids. Others believe that investment dollars and efficient organization lead to better overall wine quality. As we ponder these alternatives, let's play the game below.

Can you match these 17 large **Corporate Owner/Partners** to their 28 **Wine Properties**? If not, we've got another way for you to do it and to check your answers – **Elephant Epics, Opuses, Etc.** opposite. ⎯⎯⎯

CORPORATE OWNERS/PARTNERS

1. Piper-Heidsieck, France
2. Taittinger, France
3. Grand Metropolitan (Heublein), UK
   (Matches up with **4 Wine Properties**.)
4. Pommery, France/U.S.
5. The Wine Group (Franzia), US
6. Sanraku, Japan
7. Wine World, Inc. (Nestlé), Switz.
   (Matches up with **3 Wine Properties**.)
8. Wine World, Inc. (Nestlé)/Deutz, Switz./France
9. Teacher's Mgmt. & Invest., US
10. Suntory, Ltd., Japan
    (Matches up with **2 Wine Properties**.)
11. Isenhold, Switz.
12. Seagram Classics Wine Co., Canada
    (Matches up with **4 Wine Properties**.)
13. Eckes/Huneeus, Germany
14. Moët-Hennessy-Louis Vuitton (LVMH), France
    (Matches up with **2 Wine Properties**.)
15. A. Racke, Germany
16. Hiram Walker, Canada
    (Matches up with **2 Wine Properties**.)
17. Freixenet, Spain

WINE PROPERTIES

A. **BEAULIEU Vd.,** Rutherford
B. **BERINGER Vds.,** St. Helena
C. **BUENA VISTA W.,** Sonoma
D. **CALLAWAY Vd. and W.,** Temecula
E. **CHATEAU SOUVERAIN,** Geyserville
F. **CHATEAU ST. JEAN,** Kenwood
G. **CHRISTIAN BROS.,** St. Helena
H. **CLOS DU BOIS,** Healdsburg
I. **CORBETT CANYON,** San Luis Obispo
J. **CUVAISON,** Calistoga
K. **DOMAINE CARNEROS,** Carneros
L. **DOMAINE CHANDON,** Yountville
M. **FIRESTONE Vd.,** Los Olivos
N. **FRANCISCAN Vds.,** Rutherford
O. **SCHARFFENBERGER Cs.,** Philo
P. **GLORIA FERRER,** Sonoma
Q. **INGLENOOK,** Rutherford
R. **MAISON DEUTZ W.,** Arroyo Grande
S. **MARKHAM Vds.,** St. Helena
T. **MERIDIAN W.,** Paso Robles
U. **The MONTEREY Vd.,** Gonzales
V. **MUMM NAPA VALLEY,** Rutherford
W. **PARDUCCI W.,** Ukiah
X. **PIPER SONOMA Cs.,** Windsor
Y. **QUAIL RIDGE Cs. and Vd.,** Napa
Z. **SIMI W.,** Healdsburg
AA. **STERLING Vds.,** Calistoga
BB. **WINERY LAKE Vd.,** Carneros

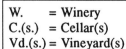

W.	= Winery
C.(s.)	= Cellar(s)
Vd.(s.)	= Vineyard(s)

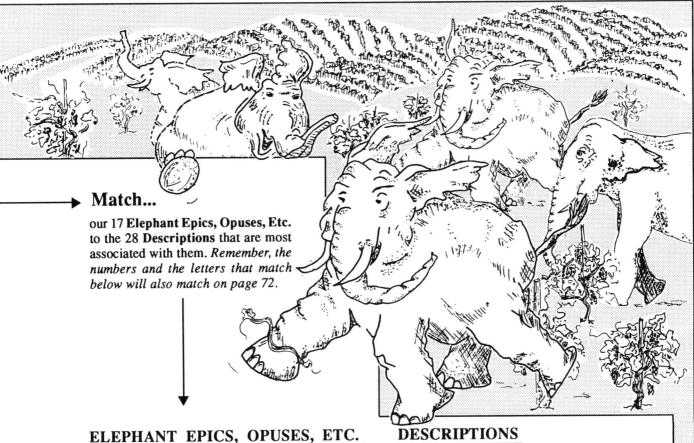

Match...

our 17 **Elephant Epics, Opuses, Etc.** to the 28 **Descriptions** that are most associated with them. *Remember, the numbers and the letters that match below will also match on page 72.*

ELEPHANT EPICS, OPUSES, ETC.

1. The city haunt of the elephaunt
2. Pachyderm-packing general
3. *...Temple Of Doom*
    (Matches up with **4 Descriptions.**)
4. *Dumbo*
5. Forbidden harvest
6. *The Elephant Man*
7. *Hatari!*
    (Matches up with **3 Descriptions.**)
8. *Jumbo*
9. *Mr. Moses*
10. *Tarzan And His Mate* (1934)
    (Matches up with **2 Descriptions.**)
11. *Jupiter's Daughter*
12. *Jungle Book*
    (Matches up with **4 Descriptions.**)
13. *The Greatest Show On Earth*
14. Babar
    (Matches up with **2 Descriptions.**)
15. *Tarzan The Ape Man* (1981)
16. Ganesh
    (Matches up with **2 Descriptions.**)
17. *Elephant Walk*

DESCRIPTIONS

A. Followed *Raiders*
B. John Wayne in business
C. Bo Derek in very little
D. Represents wisdom
E. Baby elephants marched to Mancini's music
F. Johnny Weissmuller in vines
G. Steven Spielberg in director's chair
H. Hindu elephant god
I. Ivory
J. Esther Williams in the swim of history
K. Hannibal
L. A series of children's books
M. Maureen O'Sullivan in vines
N. Charlton Heston in trouble
O. Elevated baby elephant
P. Elizabeth Taylor in trouble
Q. Harrison Ford in trouble
R. Doris Day singin' in the circus
S. John Merrick
T. Red Buttons in love
U. With elephants and a boy raised by wolves
V. Originally a book by Rudyard Kipling
W. An elephant loves con man Robert Mitchum
X. Zoo
Y. Heroine perfumes pachyderm's pate
Z. The Elephant King to kids
AA. 1942 movie with Sabu
BB. 1967 animated film

California Wine Artists

Great grapes, business acumen, and marketing techniques boost a winery's sales, but someone has to make a good product, and that is the winemaker. In Puzzle #54 below, unearth an important fact about California winemakers. In Puzzle #55, get acquainted with some winemakers and find their last names in our wordfind.

54. Warning!

Any look at winemakers and where they work is quickly outdated. Hurry and finish!
Winemakers play...

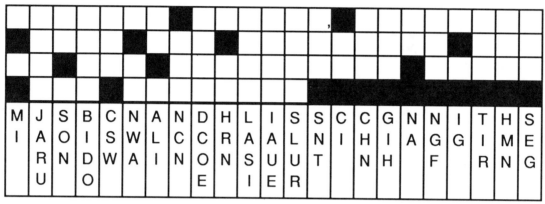

Puzzle directions are with Puzzle #17, p. 24.

55. The Artists

Well, some of them, at least. Our apologies to the many fine creators that we couldn't fit in. Our winemakers' **last names** (34 of them) are clustered around the French silver leaf corkscrew *(ca. 1750)* on the facing page. This and over 1000 other corkscrews are part of the international corkscrew collection assembled by Brother Timothy, respected winemaker emeritus of Christian Brothers Winery, St. Helena.

Richard **ARROWOOD**, *Arrowood Vds.*, Glen Ellen
Byron "Ken" **BROWN**, *Byron Vd. And W.*, Santa Maria
Cathy **CORISON**, *Chappellet*, St. Helena
Lance **CUTLER**, *Gundlach-Bundschu W.*, Vineburg
Jill **DAVIS**, *Buena Vista W., Carneros Estate*, Sonoma
Paul **DOLAN**, *Fetzer Vds.* and *Dolan Vds.*, Redwood Valley
Steve **DOOLEY**, *Edna Valley Vds.*, San Luis Obispo
Paul **DRAPER**, *Ridge Vds. & W.*, Cupertino
Bill **DYER**, *Sterling Vds.*, Calistoga
Gary **EBERLE**, *Eberle W.*, Paso Robles
Ric **FORMAN**, *Forman Vds.*, St. Helena
Randall **GRAHM**, *Bonny Doon Vd.*, Santa Cruz
Mike **GRGICH**, *Grgich Hills C.*, Rutherford
Dirk **HAMPSON**, *Far Niente*, Oakville, and *Chateau Chevalier W.*, St. Helena
Lester **HARDY**, *Cain Cs.*, St. Helena
Derek **HOLSTEIN**, *Guenoc W.*, Middletown
Randle **JOHNSON**, *Hess Collection W.*, Napa, and *Calafia Cs.*, St. Helena
Larry **LEVIN**, *Dry Creek Vd.*, Healdsburg
Zelma **LONG**, *Simi Winery*, Healdsburg, and *Long Vds.*, St. Helena
Jerry **LUPER**, (Winemaster), *Rutherford Hill W.*, Rutherford
David **MAHAFFEY**, *White Rock Vds.*, Napa
Dominic **MARTIN**, *Martin Brothers W.*, Paso Robles

W.	= Winery
C.(s.)	= Cellar(s)
Vd.(s.)	= Vineyard(s)

Michael **MARTINI**, *Louis M. Martini*, St. Helena
Justin **MEYER**, *Silver Oak Wine Cs.*, Oakville
Michael **MICHAUD**, *Chalone Vd.*, Soledad
Bill **PEASE**, *Clos Pegase W.*, Calistoga
Bernard M. **PORTET**, (por-TAY) Founding Winemaker, *Clos du Val Wine Co.*, Napa
David **RAMEY**, *Chalk Hill W.*, Healdsburg
Thomas **RINALDI**, *Duckhorn Vds.*, St. Helena
Sam **SEBASTIANI**, *Viansa W.*, Sonoma
Jed **STEELE**, *Steele Wines, Lake Co.*
Forrest **TANCER**, *Iron Horse Vds.*, Sebastopol
Alan **TENSCHER**, *Schramsberg Vds. Co.*, Calistoga
Warren **WINIARSKI**, *Stag's Leap Wine Cs.*, Napa

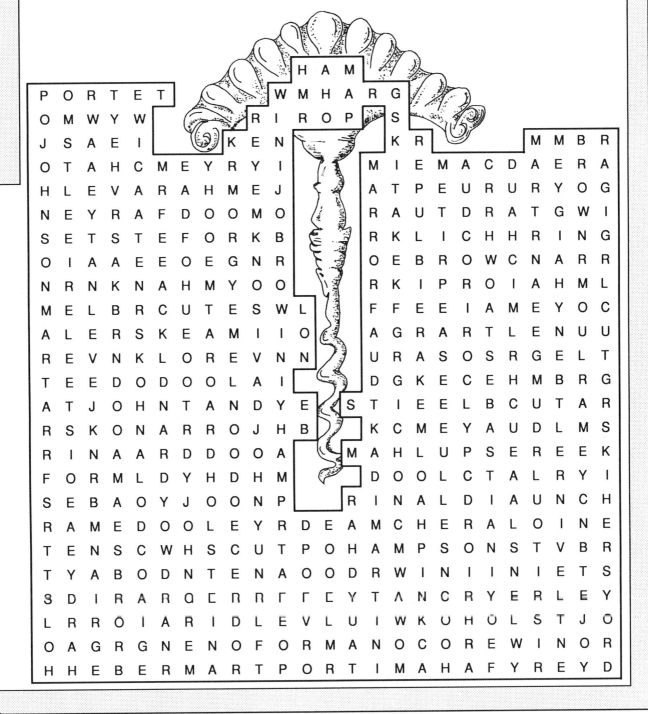

56. California Wine Labels

As the competition for your wine dollar increases, the appeal of wine labels grows, too. Besides their eye-catching beauty, wine labels present information required by a number of federal and state regulations. We've listed some **basic label regulations** below. Use these as a guide and **match our Label Descriptions (1 – 9) to their make-believe (but typical) Labels (A – I).**

Some Basic California Wine Label Regulations

Geographic Origin: If the label lists:
- *California*, then 100% of the wine's grapes were grown in the state.
- *a county* – Napa County, for example – at least 75% of the grapes were grown in that county.
- *an Official American Viticultural Area* – such as Napa Valley – it grew 85% of the grapes.
- *an individual vineyard* – i.e., "Martha's Vineyard," it's home to at least 95% of the grapes.

Kind of wine: If the label lists only:
- *a single variety* – Zinfandel, for instance – 75% of the wine comes from that grape variety.
- *a color* – "Red Table Wine," for example – or *a European name* – "Chablis," for example – or *a type name*, such as "Claret"– the wine can have any grape variety in it.

Method: If the label states:
- *Estate Bottled* – the winery and vines must both be in the stated area. The winery grows or controls grape growth and also crushes, ferments, ages, and bottles the wine in a continuous process on its property.
- *Produced And Bottled By* – the usual meaning is that at least 75% of the grapes were fermented and clarified by the bottling winery.
- *Made And Bottled By* – at least 10% of the grapes were fermented by the bottling winery.
- *Cellared And Bottled By* – the bottler didn't ferment the wine – he bought it from someone else.
- *Grown* – it's stating a non-legal term. The vintner's proud that the grapes were in his/her full care.

Vintage Date: It's printed when a least 95% of the wine's grapes were harvested and crushed in the year stated.

Alcohol: 1.5% variation is allowed if the wine is at or below 14% alcohol; a 1% variation if the wine's above.

Extra Information: Truthful data on the *percent of juice sugar at harvest* (called brix, or balling), the *percent of unfermented (residual) sugar*, and/or the *wine's total acid*, for example – are the winery's choice to add. Wineries can also create *undefined terms* like "Vintner's Reserve," and "Premium."

Label Descriptions

1 = _____

This vintage wine is from grapes grown in a vineyard that's owned by the winery, but the vineyard's not in the same viticultural area as the winery property. That's why it doesn't use the method statement "Estate Bottled." It uses the next-highest method statement.

2 = _____

A single grape variety is named on this label – so that same variety does make up a least 75% of this wine – but there's a percentage of another grape variety in there.

3 = _____

This wine is named after a famous French Chardonnay region. However, instead of Chardonnay, it's made from a variety of less-noble white grapes of different years and from separated areas in the state.

4 = _____

This label states a single vineyard, so you know that at least 95% of the grapes came from there.

5 = _____

This wine was fully made by the winery named on the label, but the grapes came from another state.

6 = _____

This wine was made by someone other than the firm listed on the label. Its grapes were harvested in different years and from different areas.

7 = _____

This proud vintner wanted you to know that he/she did it all.

8 = _____

This vintner bought 90% and fermented 10% of the wine from 2 noble Rhône grape varieties harvested in the same year from widely separated vineyards. Since neither grape variety constituted 75% of the wine, she couldn't use just 1 varietal name on the label.

9 = _____

This wine blends grapes from 2 different areas. It adds a non-legal term than can mean anything.

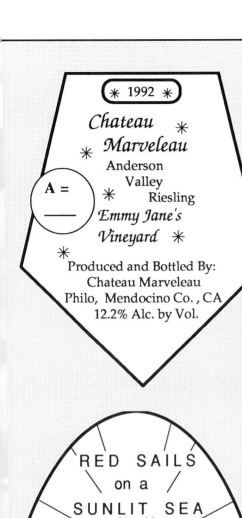

* 1992 *

Chateau Marveleau
Anderson Valley Riesling
Emmy Jane's Vineyard

A = ____

Produced and Bottled By:
Chateau Marveleau
Philo, Mendocino Co., CA
12.2% Alc. by Vol.

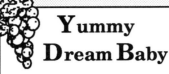

Yummy Dream Baby

A California Red Table Wine
1992
Made and Bottled by
Domaine Vinifera
Cupertino CA
12.5 % Alc. by vol.

B = ____

70% Grenache 30% Mourvedre

WWC

Estate Bottled

Sonoma County
Chardonnay
1992

C = ____

Grown, Produced, and Bottled By
Wonderous Wine Co., Inc.
Healdsburg, CA 11.5% Alc. by Vol.

Spectacular **V**ineyards

D = ____

Private
Reserve   1993

47% Lake County
53% Sonoma County

SAUVIGNON BLANC

Produced And Bottled By
Spectacular Vineyards
Lakeport, Lake Co. CA
11.5% Alcohol by Volume

RED SAILS
on a
SUNLIT SEA

F = ____

California
Red Table Wine

Cellared & Bottled By:
Guacamole Enterprises, Lodi, CA
11.3% Alcohol By Vol.

Loveus
Family
Winery

E = ____

AMADOR COUNTY
Zinfandel

1990
Produced & Bottled
By The
Loveus Winery
Napa, Calif.
Alcohol 13% by Vol.

BIG COMPANY

CALIFORNIA
CHABLIS

A Light, Crisp
White Wine

G = ____

Produced & Bottled By Big Co.
Modesto, CA USA
Alcohol 9% By Vol.

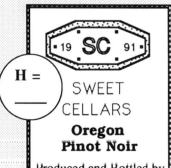

· 19 **SC** 91 ·

H = ____

SWEET
CELLARS
Oregon Pinot Noir

Produced and Bottled by
Sweet Cellars
Richmond, California
Alcohol 12.9% by vol.

Estate (*1989*) Bottled

FABULOUS WINERY

NAPA VALLEY

Cabernet Sauvignon

I = ____

PRODUCED & BOTTLED
BY
FABULOUS WINERY, ST. HELENA
NAPA CALIFORNIA USA
ALCOHOL 12.5% BY VOLUME

Front Label

The grapes in this wonderful, tasty wine came from our own Fabulous vineyards in famous Napa Valley. This scrumptious wine's sugar at harvest was 22.5% by weight. Total acidity: 0.78% by volume. It was lovingly aged for 3 years in precious French Limousin oak barrels as the sweet, warm sun and pale, magical moon shone on our winery-tasting room-art museum-amphitheater-cooking school-restaurant-classic car collection-arboretum-skyway-train station complex nestled here in our quiet, jeweled valley.

9% Merlot grapes soften this phenomenal wine. It's ready to drink tonight, or age it 3 years. I hope you buy 20 cases.

Glen Gifted, Winemaker

Back Label

57. Washington And Oregon

Investigate two emerging, already respected wine regions. Match our **Winners (1 – 11)** to **Their Deeds Or Awards (A – K)**. That will also match Oregonian and Washingtonian **Wine Areas (1 – 11 on the map)** to their **Wine Area Descriptions (A – K)** on the facing page. Learn about them now: they're getting more important as we speak.

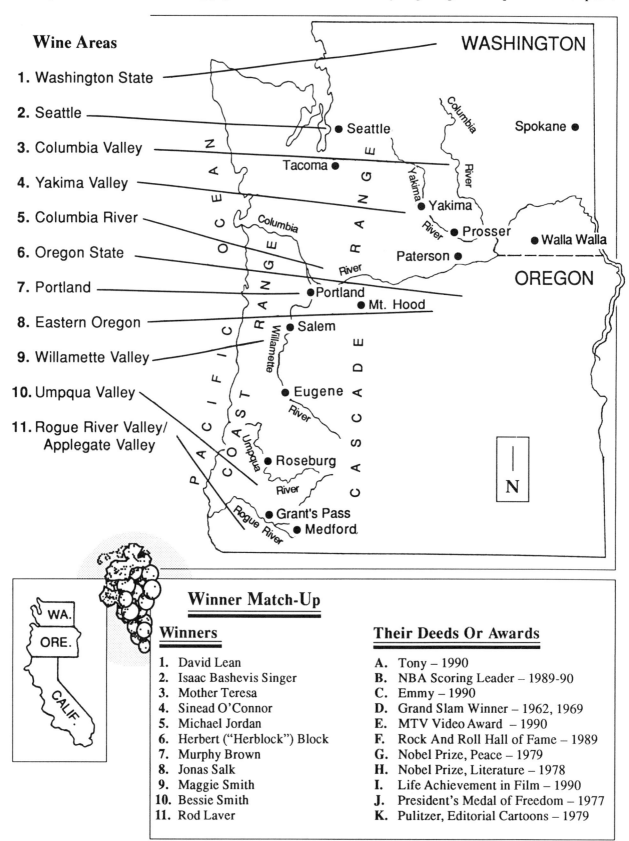

Wine Areas

1. Washington State
2. Seattle
3. Columbia Valley
4. Yakima Valley
5. Columbia River
6. Oregon State
7. Portland
8. Eastern Oregon
9. Willamette Valley
10. Umpqua Valley
11. Rogue River Valley/
    Applegate Valley

Winner Match-Up

Winners	Their Deeds Or Awards
1. David Lean	A. Tony – 1990
2. Isaac Bashevis Singer	B. NBA Scoring Leader – 1989-90
3. Mother Teresa	C. Emmy – 1990
4. Sinead O'Connor	D. Grand Slam Winner – 1962, 1969
5. Michael Jordan	E. MTV Video Award – 1990
6. Herbert ("Herblock") Block	F. Rock And Roll Hall of Fame – 1989
7. Murphy Brown	G. Nobel Prize, Peace – 1979
8. Jonas Salk	H. Nobel Prize, Literature – 1978
9. Maggie Smith	I. Life Achievement in Film – 1990
10. Bessie Smith	J. President's Medal of Freedom – 1977
11. Rod Laver	K. Pulitzer, Editorial Cartoons – 1979

Wine Area Descriptions

A. Oregon's principal (and coolest) growing spot. **WINE AREA #** _____

B. The irrigation lifeline of both states' eastern vineyards. **WINE AREA #** _____

C. Main city of Oregon's main wine territory. **WINE AREA #** _____

D. These valleys and river near the California border are a bit warmer than the two valleys to the north. Valley View Winery is here. **WINE AREA #** _____

E. This land is named after its Indian nation owners and is a part of the larger Columbia Valley. It's home to newer wineries that are close to the vineyards. *Vinifera* were first planted here in the late 1800's. **WINE AREA #** _____

F. This district receives less rain than the valley to the north. Oregon's first *vinifera* vines since Prohibition were planted here. **WINE AREA #** _____

G. Almost all of Washington's vineyards lie here, east of the Cascade Mountains. That range protects the vines against the west coast's heavy rain. Indeed, this country is an arid near-desert that depends on irrigation. Long, hot days and very cool nights slow-ripen the grapes – Cabernet Sauvignon, Merlot, and various white varieties. This appellation includes Yakima Valley, Walla Walla Valley, and the newer Paterson district, then it splashes down into Oregon. **WINE AREA #** _____

H. This is the location of many of Washington's older wineries, over 150 miles west of the vineyards. **WINE AREA #** _____

I. This region grows the U.S.'s second largest (California grows the largest) amount of *vinifera* plants. Its white wines show strong fruit and good acidity; its reds have balance and finesse. Chief grapes: white Riesling, Chardonnay, Chenin Blanc, Sauvignon Blanc, Sémillon, Gewürztraminer, and Muscat Canelli, and red Cabernet Sauvignon, Merlot, and the Austrian Lemberger. 80+ wineries are here, the largest being Chateau Ste. Michelle, who owns about 50% of state plantings. Some other wineries: Arbor Crest, Columbia Winery, E. B. Foote, Preston, F. W. Langguth, Covey Run, Yakima River, Manfred Vierthaler, Hinzerling, Mont Elise, Hogue, Stewart, Woodward Canyon, and Snoqualmie. **WINE AREA #** _____

J. The state with its chief vineyards in the west eventually started vineyards and wineries in this dry, warm, eastern belt. **WINE AREA #** _____

K. This place makes wines known for their subtlety – one side effect of rainy, cool weather. Rain, especially at harvest time, is always a concern. Much wine from here is made with grapes grown by Region A above, but a bright future, especially for its home-grown Pinot Noir, is hoped for by wine folks everywhere, including the French Burgundy firm, Joseph Drouhin, who owns Pinot Noir vineyards here. Chief grapes are cool-weather, early-ripening ones: the red Pinot Noir, and the whites Chardonnay, Riesling, Pinot Gris, Gewürztraminer, and Müller-Thurgau, plus a little Cabernet Sauvignon, Merlot, and Sauvignon Blanc. Almost all 70+ wineries are small; the more well-known are: Amity, Elk Cove, Eyrie, Knudsen-Erath (this state's largest winery), Ponzi, Sokol Blosser, Tualatin, Valley View. **WINE AREA #** _____

DAFFY DEFINITION: Umpqua – a sound emitted by a tuba.

58. Washington And Oregon II

Recap the chief wine areas of these 2 states by playing this game. First, take a minute to notice our game design. It's based on western Washington's Paterson district. That area is known for its unique circular fields. Non-grape crops were often cultivated in such circles, and the same shape was extended to grapevines. Mark Jennings of Château Ste. Michelle/Columbia Crest says that an irrigating arm used to extend from each circle's center to a wheel that ran around the circumference. Today, however, vintners choose drip irrigation and lay their new vineyards in conventional rows.

Eight of our circular vineyards have blocks of letters in them. **Hiding in each block are adjoining letters that connect to form a word, as in Circle #1.** Cultivate the rest of these, place your words on their matching-numbered blanks, and read a summary of Washington and Oregon grapegrowing.

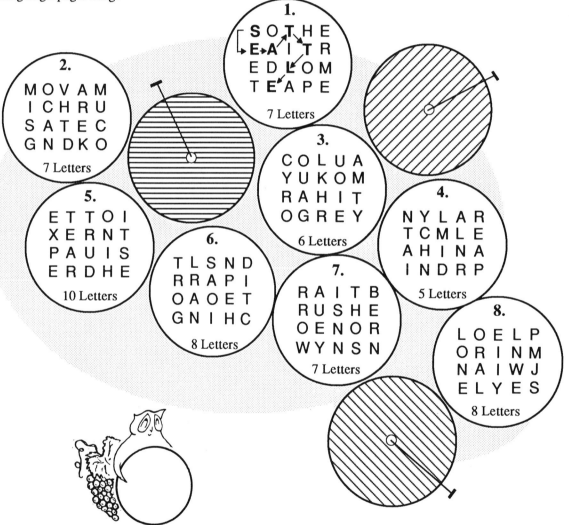

1.
S O T H E
E A I T R
E D L O M
T E A P E
7 Letters

2.
M O V A M
I C H R U
S A T E C
G N D K O
7 Letters

3.
C O L U A
Y U K O M
R A H I T
O G R E Y
6 Letters

4.
N Y L A R
T C M L E
A H I N A
I N D R P
5 Letters

5.
E T T O I
X E R N T
P A U I S
E R D H E
10 Letters

6.
T L S N D
R R A P I
O A O E T
G N I H C
8 Letters

7.
R A I T B
R U S H E
O E N O R
W Y N S N
7 Letters

8.
L O E L P
O R I N M
N A I W J
E L Y E S
8 Letters

Washington's wineries used to stay west of the Cascades, close to cool (1 **SEATTLE**   . They (2_____ in grapes from hot vineyards that lay 150 miles east across the Cascades, near Walla Walla, Spokane, Paterson, and in the (3_____ Valley. Now, wineries bloom in those eastern vineyards. Both Chateau Ste. Michelle and California's growing Chalone corporation are planting Paterson's new, (4_____ Canoe Ridge area.

Oregon's older winegrowing (5_____, and its chief wineries and vineyards, still radiate south from rainy (6_____, along the cool (7_____ slopes of the Cascades. Over the Cascades to the hot east, a few (8_____ and many vineyards extend along the south side of the Columbia River.

59. New York Grapes

New York is second to California in U.S. wine production. However, California's fine wines come from only one grape species – the European *Vitis vinifera* (usually grafted onto American rootstock.) New York grows 3 different species and each New York winery chooses which species it will cultivate and produce. Take a look at the grapes New Yorkers pick from. (Some pun intended.)

The words in Section #1 are in order, **the lines themselves are not in order**. Follow punctuation and other clues and get them in shape. Do the same with II, III, and IV.

I. Native American *Vitis labrusca* grapes

1. New York's sweet, sparkling, jug, and
2. taste that's called "foxy." Some native
3. York's cruel winters and hot
4. and Elvira, and pinkish Delaware.
5. grapes are: the red Catawba and
6. These hardy grape vines withstand New
7. kosher wines. As varietals, *labrusca*
8. Concord (New York grows more Concord
9. summers. They're the backbone of
10. wines give a strong, gamey odor and
11. than any other grape), white Niagara

II. *Vitis vinifera* grapes

1. *vinifera* grapes (Chardonnay,
2. to grow in New York's harsh
3. successfully grew and made fine
4. are slowly giving them a try.
5. The classic European *vitis*
6. 1950's, Dr. Konstantin Frank
7. Riesling, etc.) always failed
8. climate. However, in the
9. wines from them: now others

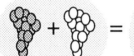

III. Hybrid grapes

1. Blanc, Cayuga, Aurora, and Vignoles, and the red Maréchal Foch,
2. where in between native *labrusca* and *vinifera*. How? The French
3. York continues to develop those crosses and to create new
4. crossbred the two species and developed several hybrids. New
5. Baco Noir, and Chelois.
6. Most New York winemakers believe that their future rests some-
7. ones. The object is to marry *vinifera's* taste with *labrusca's*
8. strength. Some popular hybrids are: white Seyval Blanc, Vidal

IV. So...

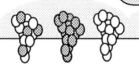

1. hybrid and vinifera wines. Hargrave
2. Great Western Co., for example, down-
3. to their climates and markets. The large
4. and hybrid and *labrusca* sparkling
5. New York wineries grow and use
6. wines. Popular Rivendell Winery
7. plays *vinifera* and makes hybrid varietals
8. all of these 3 types of grapes according
9. avoids *labrusca* and specializes in
10. Vineyard concentrates on *vinifera* only.

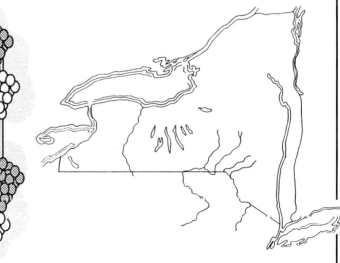

DAFFY DEFINITION: Hybrids! – A casual salutation on meeting Seyval Blanc or Maréchal Foch vines.

60. New York Wine Areas

Figure out New York's 4 major winegrowing regions. Areas #1, 2, 3, and 4 display **visual clues** and they start off their **Descriptions** with **verbal clues**. Read each **Clue and Description** carefully!

Area #1 Clues and Description.

The actress Veronica would have used both eyes to see this lovely area better, and it wouldn't have made her feel icky, or weird, or strange. This region, with its important Chautauqua district, raises mostly Concord (Concord here makes up about one-half of New York's grape acreage), plus hybrid grapes and a little *vinifera*. These are used by local wineries and sold to many producers in Area #3. Wineries: F. S. Johnson Vds., Merritt Estate, Woodbury.

Area #1 Name = _____ _____

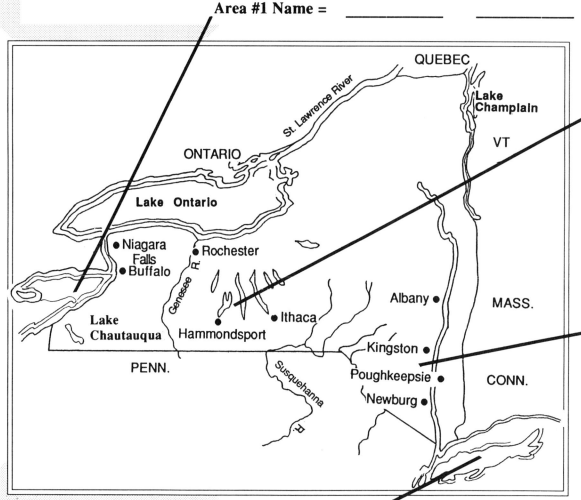

Area #2 Clues and Description.

John Silver couldn't have unearthed a more exciting treasure on a body of land completely surrounded by water than the newest New York wine spot. The surrounding ocean and longer growing season foster sophisticated *vinifera* wines from Chardonnay, Sauvignon Blanc, Cabernet Sauvignon, Pinot Noir, Merlot, Riesling, and Gewürztraminer. Some wineries: Hargrave, Gristina, Lenz, Bedell, Pindar, Bridgehampton, Palmer, Peconic Bay, Mattituck Hills, Jamesport.

Area #2 Name = _____ _____

Area #3 Clues and Description.

One digit couldn't count the winemaking milestones that characterize this prime glacier-carved wine territory. We doubt not that Veronica and her sisters would want to learn it all. Here is the home of giant Canandaigua Wine, seller of 15 million cases annually – 98% from purchased grapes – and little giant Taylor Wine Co. It's also the lair of iconoclastic Walter S. Taylor (Bully Hill), who specializes in old-fashioned *labrusca* and hybrid wines, and is the master of off-beat, defiant labels. Here's the historic spot (Gold Seal) where Charles Fournier encouraged Dr. Konstantin Frank to develop New York's first viable *vinifera*. Other noted wineries: Glenora, Great Western, Heron Hill, Wagner, Widmer's, Hermann J. Wiemer, and Dr. Frank's Vinifera Wine Cellars. This area is highlighted on the bottom of this page.

Area #3 Name = _____ _____

Area #4 Clues and Description.

Rumor has it that a famous British detective wanted to send his landlady here to buy wines, but he imagined the large, swiftly-moving stream of tears that the locals would produce when it was time for her to return to England. He visualized them singing to her, *"From this elongated depression of the earth's surface, usually between ranges of hills, they say you are leaving..."* and he decided to spare their sorrow and keep her at home. This historic strip is celebrated as the oldest winegrowing district in the U.S. About 75 miles north of New York City, it supports 20+ wineries who specialize in French-American hybrids, with some *vinifera*. Wineries: Benmarl, North Salem, Valley, Rivendell.

Area #4 Name = _____ _____ _____

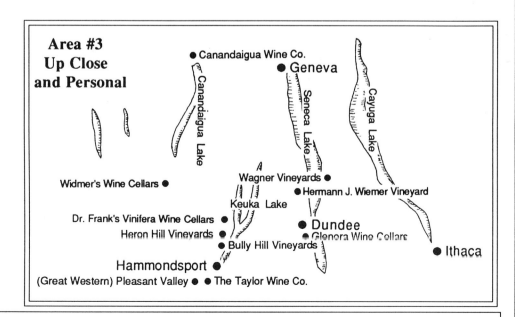

Area #3 Up Close and Personal

- ● Canandaigua Wine Co.
- ● Geneva
- Canandaigua Lake
- Seneca Lake
- Cayuga Lake
- Widmer's Wine Cellars ●
- Wagner Vineyards ●
- ● Hermann J. Wiemer Vineyard
- Keuka Lake
- Dr. Frank's Vinifera Wine Cellars ●
- ● Dundee
- Heron Hill Vineyards ●
- ● Glenora Wine Cellars
- ● Bully Hill Vineyards
- ● Ithaca
- Hammondsport ●
- (Great Western) Pleasant Valley ● ● The Taylor Wine Co.

DAFFY DEFINITION: Riesling – a fledgling, or infant, Ries. (Rieses are quite loving parents to their lings.)

61. There, Too?

Yes! Yes! Yes! Other states are proud of their wines. Be sure to sample them when you travel through. For now, just put these wine-producing states into their correct boxes.

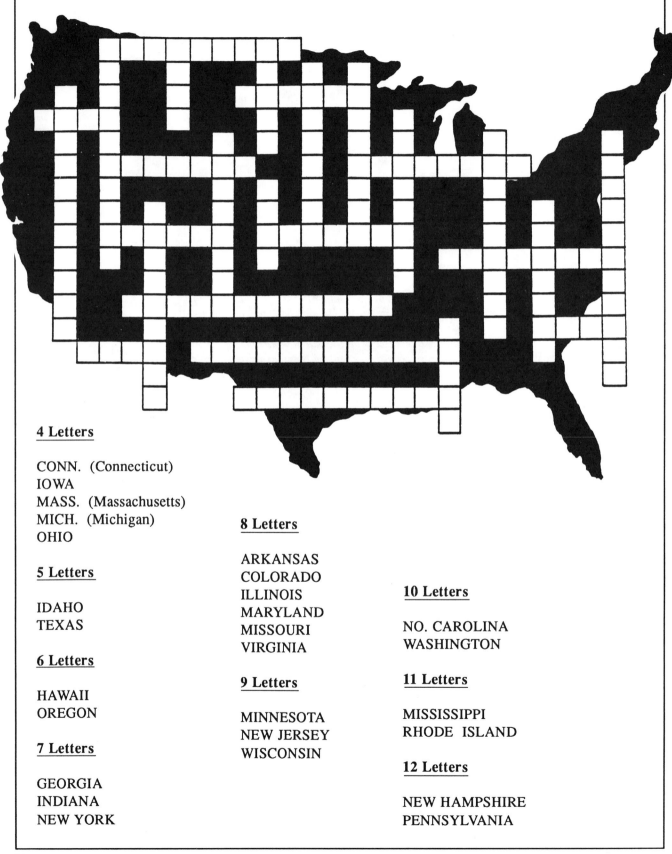

4 Letters

CONN. (Connecticut)
IOWA
MASS. (Massachusetts)
MICH. (Michigan)
OHIO

5 Letters

IDAHO
TEXAS

6 Letters

HAWAII
OREGON

7 Letters

GEORGIA
INDIANA
NEW YORK

8 Letters

ARKANSAS
COLORADO
ILLINOIS
MARYLAND
MISSOURI
VIRGINIA

9 Letters

MINNESOTA
NEW JERSEY
WISCONSIN

10 Letters

NO. CAROLINA
WASHINGTON

11 Letters

MISSISSIPPI
RHODE ISLAND

12 Letters

NEW HAMPSHIRE
PENNSYLVANIA

Our North American wine excursions — through California, Washington, Oregon, and New York – are finished. As we have learned, many North American grapes, wine types, and wine methods originated in Europe. Pull out your passports! We're off to some of the countries that started it all – France, Germany, Italy, Spain, and Portugal. We'll also visit Australia and South America, two other New World wine producers that owe a debt to Europe.

We should note that the New World has returned the favor. It exported back into Europe the skills of modern winemaking technology and a lively spirit of innovation. This New World creativity is revitalizing many Old World wine traditions.

Voltaire

Which man said which quotation?
_____

Wine is...the divine juice of September.

Wine is...the first weapon that devils use.

St. Jerome

Yes, St. Jerome is credited with the second quote. He sounds disparaging, but we suspect that he was quoted out of context. Besides, now that he's a saint, he knows better.

62. French Fortune

Travel with us through France's major wine regions. Each **Clue** on the facing page gives hints about the wine region, river, or city it describes. **Use a Clue and the map to identify the wine location, then fill its name onto the provided blanks.** When you finish filling in all the blanks, tackle the puzzle at the bottom of the facing page.

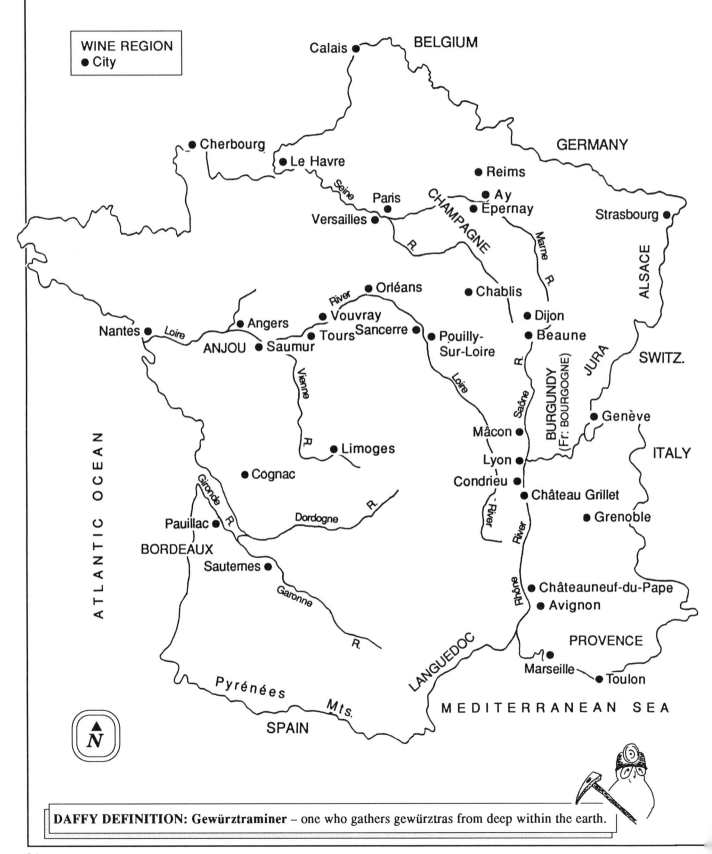

WINE REGION
● City

BELGIUM
Calais
GERMANY
Cherbourg
Le Havre
Reims
Seine
Ay
Paris
CHAMPAGNE
Épernay
Versailles
R.
Marne R.
Strasbourg
ALSACE
Orléans
Chablis
River
Vouvray
Dijon
Angers
Tours
Sancerre
Beaune
Nantes
Loire
Pouilly-
Sur-Loire
ANJOU
Saumur
R.
JURA
SWITZ.
Vienne
Saône R.
BURGUNDY
(Fr: BOURGOGNE)
R.
Mâcon
Genève
ATLANTIC OCEAN
Limoges
Lyon
ITALY
Cognac
Condrieu
Château Grillet
River
Grenoble
Gironde R.
Dordogne
R.
Pauillac
BORDEAUX
Rhône
Sauternes
Châteauneuf-du-Pape
Garonne
Avignon
R.
Rhône
PROVENCE
Pyrénées
LANGUEDOC
Marseille
Toulon
Mts.
MEDITERRANEAN SEA
SPAIN
N

DAFFY DEFINITION: Gewürztraminer – one who gathers gewürztras from deep within the earth.

Clues:

1. Folks here speak a form of German. They fashion popular, firm, dry, fragrant whites chiefly from the Riesling and Gewürztraminer grapes. Contrary to most French practices, these wines are named after their grape varieties instead of after their birthplace.

— — — — [1] —

2. The wines along this river valley are usually red, such as those of Côte Rôtie, Hermitage, and Châteauneuf-du-Pape. They do, however, include the famous white appellations of Condrieu and Château Grillet.

— [2] — — —

3. This river port creates celebrated red clarets, dry white Graves wines, Sauternes (the world's most famous sweet white), and Château Pétrus, one of the world's most expensive reds.

— — — — — [3] — —

4. This chief seaport is where the river of Region #2 empties.

[4] — — — — — — —

5. This province is known more for its Riviera playground than for its wine. The Bandol district near Toulon is acknowledged for its Mourvèdre grape red wines. (Pay attention to this clue!)

[5] — — — — —

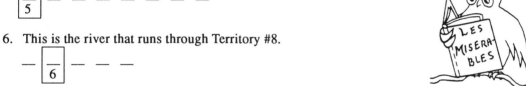

6. This is the river that runs through Territory #8.

— [6] — — —

7. Also called the Midi (or South) this huge, ancient wine province is still known for its overproduction of very ordinary red wines. Better grapes and a growing interest in fine winemaking are slowly altering that image.

— — — [7] — — — —

8. Producing world-class food and wines (reds from the Pinot Noir, and whites from Chardonnay and Pinot Blanc), this tradition-rich, former duchy stretches south from Dijon to Lyon. It includes the Chablis zone that is offset to the northwest.

— — — — — [8] — —

9. This river, France's longest, flows past a cornucopia of wines. They include: Nantes's Muscadet; Anjou's *Cabernet de Anjou* rosés; Saumur's dry and sparkling Chenin Blancs and Cabernet Franc reds; Vouvray's myriad styles of Chenin Blancs; and Pouilly-Fumé, a fine dry wine style made from Sauvignon Blanc.

— — — — [9]

Did you find them all? Good! Now, place the boxed letters above onto their matching-numbered blanks below. You'll spell out the name of another important French wine area.

10. Other countries try to duplicate this Marne River wine. Germany's versions are called "*sekt;*" Italy names its styles "*spumante.*"

— — — — — — — — —
  1   2   3   4   5   6   7   8   9

63. German Gold

Our map is missing names of 10 key German wine regions. How will you fill them in? We've done one to start you off.* Each of the 10 Regions on the facing page is next to a math problem. Problem G's solution is 9. We wrote G's Region – Mittelrhein – on the #9 blank on the **map** and now we know where Mittelrhein is located. Then we wrote "Mittelrhein" on the #9 blank in our **Region Descriptions** list and learned more about it. Holy Blue Nun! You can locate each region and read about it, too!

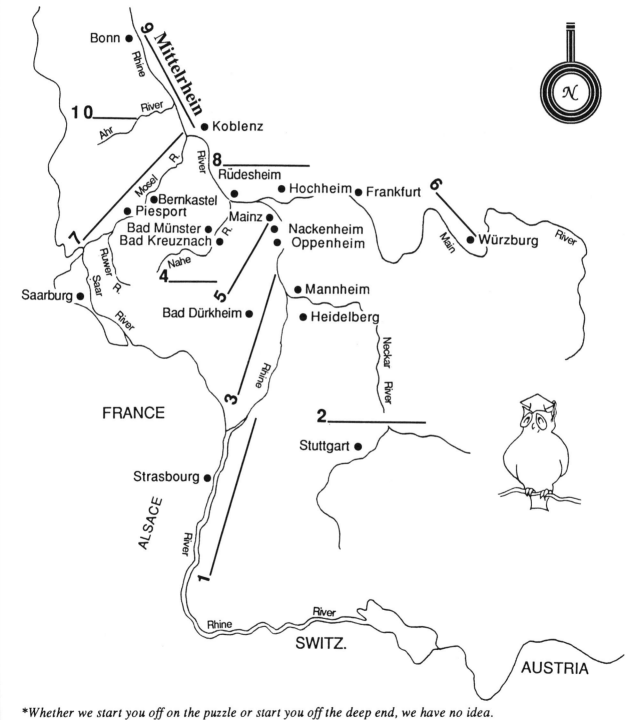

Whether we start you off on the puzzle or start you off the deep end, we have no idea.

DAFFY DEFINITION: Bad Münster – a town that's evidently as naughty as Bad Kreuznach.

Regions

A. Rheinpfalz ....7 + 343 x 9 – 3,148 + 1 = ___

B. Franken ....6 + 456 x 7 – 439 + 5 – 2,794 = ___

C. Baden ....10 x 11 ÷ 2 ÷ 5 – 1 ÷ 5 – 1 = ___

D. Nahe ....24 – 3 + 9 x 2 – 25 x 3 – 101 = ___

E. Württemberg.............58 ÷ 2 – 7 ÷ 11 = ___

F. Rheinhessen..............17 – 3 + 1 x 3 – 40 = ___

G. Mittelrhein ....126 ÷ 9 x 2 – 19 = __9__

H. Mosel-Saar-Ruwer ...98 ÷ 7 – 7 = ___

I. Rheingau ....27 x 2 ÷ 6 – 1 = ___

J. Ahr ....200 ÷ 10 – 20 + 10 = ___

Region Descriptions

1. _____ This Black Forest zone is close to Alsace, France. Its wines come from white Müller-Thurgau, Pinot Gris, Riesling, Gewürztraminer, and Silvaner grapes, and from red Spätburgunder (Pinot Noir) grapes.

2. _____ Red grapes form half of this Neckar River territory's plantings, with the native Trollinger grape as a specialty. The people here have been called Swabians from ancient times.

3. _____ Germany's sunniest and second-largest wine acreage used to supply the Holy Roman Empire with its wines. Müller-Thurgau is the most planted of many varieties here, but Riesling, as is the case in much of Germany, makes the most praised wines.

4. _____ Appreciated for its complex Rieslings, this small district's most famous vineyards are the *Bastei* in Bad Münster, the *Kupfergrube* ('copper mine') in Schlossböckelheim, and the *Kahlenberg* in Bad Kreuznach.

5. _____ Germany's largest acreage produces mostly light, ordinary wines. Much is blended by cooperatives into Liebfraumilch ('Blessed Mother's Milk'), a simple, sweetish product. Its few fine Riesling producers overlook the Rhine river and cluster near the villages of Nierstein, Oppenheim, and Nackenheim.

6. _____ Müller-Thurgau grapes make up more than half of this area's acreage, but this Main River region is especially famous for its wonderful Silvaner wines, full, dry, and flavor-filled. These liquids go into a round, flat-sided bottle, the *Bocksbeutel,* a legally protected 'trademark' of the area.

7. _____ Three rivers name this region, beloved for its subtle, scented, scintillating Rieslings. Some wine lovers judge them to be lighter, more refined and fragrant than Rieslings made along the Rhine itself. Its more famous vineyards: *Goldtröpfchen* (Little Gold Drop) in Piesport and steep-sided *Doctor* in Bernkastel. Müller-Thurgau grapes make up this territory's lesser wines.

8. _____ This place is extolled as the birthplace of some of the world's greatest white wines. Its vineyards run along the Rhine's north bank, with excellent exposure and river warmth: its rich, balanced, complex, mostly Riesling wines inspire poetry and speechless contemplation. Among its famous vineyards: *Schloss Johannisberg, Schloss Vollrads,* and *Steinberg.*

9. __Mittelrhein__ This narrow, castle-bedecked region makes chiefly Riesling wines.

10. _____ A small wine district (Germany's northernmost) that produces velvety red wines made from Spätburgunder (Pinot Noir) grapes.

64. Italian Treasure

Land of wine! That's what the Greeks named Italy, and all of Italy's 20 geographic regions prove the name: together they produce more wine quantity and variety than any country in the world. **We've picked 12 of those regions** and written 12 **Region Descriptions** of them on the facing page. However, none of the Region Descriptions says which of the 12 regions it's describing! How will you know? The shapes of our 12 regions surround our map. They've been turned upside down and all around, but we cleverly saw that Shape #12 is the same shape as Sardinia, so we know that Region Description #12 tells about the island Sardinia and its wines. Look sharply and you can follow our example with the other 11 regions and match each Region to its Region Description.

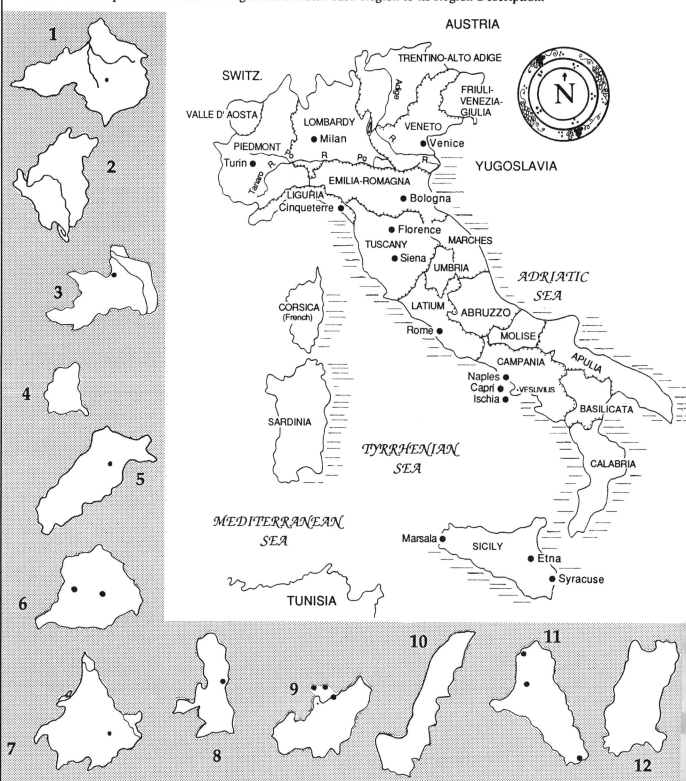

Region Descriptions

1. _____This is the mountain home of famous red Nebbiolo grape wines - part of Italy's wine nobility. Some respected Nebbiolo producers reside in the districts of Barbaresco and Barolo. In addition, Barbera, Dolcetto, Freisa, and Grignolino grapes create an exciting array of still or fizzy, fresh and fruity, or complex and hard wines, and popular Asti *spumante* (sparkling wine). California plants Nebbiolo and Barbera.

2. _____This area is marked by the German language, professional wine production, varietal labeling, sparkling wines, light reds and rosés (especially from the native Schiava grape), and white wines.

3. _____This land of Romeo and Juliet houses the Soave district's young, dry, softly blended whites and the Valpolicella area's fresh, soft, fruity blended reds. Two specialities made from air-dried grapes are dry, rich *Amarone* wines and sweet, rich *Recioto* wines. This region uses some varietal labeling such as with Merlot and Cabernet Franc and it hosts Italy's viticultural research center at Conegliano.

4. _____The often excellent wines here are labeled by grape variety – Pinot Grigio, Merlot, Cabernet Franc, Pinot Bianco, Chardonnay, and Cabernet Sauvignon, for example.

5. _____Not known for great wines, this region creates marvelous food and the world-popular, fruity, slightly sparkling Lambrusco wines. It's the headquarters of the Riunite firm. (*"Riunite on ice...tastes nice..."*).

6. _____This is the hilly, aristocratic homeland of the Sangiovese grape and its famous wine, Chianti. Three popular versions of Chianti are: fresh and frizzante (slightly sparkling); warm, fragrant, and aged (Riservas); and newer styles, sometimes with "foreign" Cabernet Sauvignon mixed in.

7. _____The Valtellina Valley near the Swiss border makes good, dry reds from the Nebbiolo grape.(There it's called Chiavennasca). The Oltrepò Pavese area, north of the Po River, uses Barbera for its reds and it fashions sparkling wines from Pinot Bianco and Pinot Grigio grapes.

8. _____Soft, white, drinkable whites made with Trebbiano and Malvasia grapes characterize this territory. Most familiar are the wines of the Castelli Romani district, southeast of Rome. These include wines from the villages of Frascati and Marino and from the Colli Lanuvini and Colli Albani zones. The poetically named, but simple white wine, *Est! Est!! Est!!! di Montefiascone* is from here, too.

9. _____Most wines from here don't inspire admiration, but this region of Mt. Vesuvio and Capri Island boasts several notable exceptions, including red Taurasi, an Aglianico/Sangiovese grape blend.

10. _____This most productive of all Italian wine regions makes mostly blending wine, but it's developing some appreciated table wines. One of its chief grapes is the Primitivo, believed by ampelographers* (grape investigators) to be the same as California's versatile Zinfandel.

11. _____Another old zone that's quickly modernizing, it produces great quantities of blending wine and is creating better (mostly white) table wines. Some enjoyable reds and rosés come from the volcanic earth near Mr. Etna, and Italy's famous fortified wine, *Marsala*, is born in the city of the same name.

12. __SARDINIA_____Known in the past for sweet Malvasia and Moscato wine and also for dry, sherry-like *Vernaccia di Oristano*, this area's modern firms are now making increasingly good table wines.

Italian Names
Apulia = Pulia
Latium = Lazio
Lombardy = Lombardia
Marches = Marche
Piedmont = Piemonte
Sicily = Sicilia
Sardinia = Sardegna
Tuscany = Toscana
Vesuvius = Vesuvio

*Ampelographer hard at work.

DAFFY DEFINITION: Po – (Southern U.S. idiom) to transfer wine from one container (i.e., bottle) to another (i.e., glass). "Mayah po yawl s'morah wahn?"

65. Spanish Sorcery

Spain has the greatest acreage devoted to the vine, but primitive methods keep crop levels low, so Spain is behind Italy and France in actual wine production. Several families and firms are aggressively pulling their regions into the modern winemaking age. There's always something new happening in Spanish wine development.

Fill 9 Spanish wine regions onto our map. Match our 9 **Spanish Notables (A – I)** to their **Descriptions (1 – 9)**. That will also match the **blanks on our map (A – I)** to their **Wine Regions And Descriptions (1 – 9)**. *!Bien Viaje!*

Spanish Notables

A. Generalissimo Francisco Franco

B. Catherine

C. Javier Pérez de Cuellar

D. Pablo Picasso

E. Teresa

F. Rodrigo Díaz de Vivar

G. Isabella

H. Salvador Dali

I. Miguel de Cervantes Saavedra

Spanish Notables Descriptions

1. El Cid, great medieval general

2. Columbus depended on this one.

3. His *"Persistence of Memory"* melted watches.

4. His *Don Quixote* ridiculed romance novels.

5. Perpetually deceased on *Saturday Night Live* T.V.

6. United Nations Secretary General, 1982–1991

7. This one was a brainy mystic in Ávila.

8. Henry VIII divorced this one.

9. His *"Guernica"* cried out against war.

Wine Regions and Descriptions

1. **Navarra** .... This old, royal land turns Garnacha (Grenache) and Tempranillo grapes into well-liked dry rosés and reds in the lighter Rioja style. **AREA** _____

2. **Rioja** .... Spain's most famous table wines flow from this high, mountainous land. Its reds, from Tempranillo, Garnacha, Mazuelo, and Graciano grapes, display an historical Bordeaux touch. Its whites are from Viura, Garnacha Blanca, and Malvasia grapes. **AREA** _____

3. **Penedés** .... This district creates admirable reds and 90% of Spain's sparkling wine, the best of which are world-class. Its growing vineyards include internationally favorite grapes – Chardonnay, Cabernet Sauvignon, Sauvignon Blanc, etc., in addition to native varieties such as the Garnacha and Tempranillo. **AREA** _____

4. **Ribera del Duero** ... This area is praised for its red wines, made chiefly from Tempranillo, Garnacha, Cabernet Sauvignon, and Merlot. **AREA** _____

5. **Rueda** .... Wine experts admire the full, dry white wines that this hot zone is starting to make with modern white winemaking techniques. Chief grapes: Verdejo and Viura. **AREA** _____

6. **Valdepeñas** .... Most of La Mancha's Valdepeñas district wines are blends of wines from the white Airén and the red Tempranillo (here called Cencibel) grapes. Drunk young, they're considered fruity and appealing. **AREA** _____

7. **Montilla – Moriles** .... This is the home of Montilla wines made from Pedro Ximénes grapes. These wines are similar to sherry, but they're more naturally high in alcohol, so they're not always fortified. Montilla wines are fermented in large clay jars *(tinajas)*. **AREA** _____

8. **Málaga** .... This city gave its name to famous deep, sweet, fortified wines made from Moscatel grapes. Pedro Ximénes grapes make lighter, drier Málaga wines. **AREA** _____

9. **Jerez de la Frontera** .... The English "adjusted" this city's Spanish name and called the city and its fortified, long-aged, blended wines "sherry." Jerez is the center of this tradition-filled wine industry. Chief grapes are the Palomino and Pedro Ximénes. **AREA** _____

93

66. Portugal's Palette

Portugal is especially known for rosé, Madeira, and port wines. In addition to these, most Portuguese enjoy red and white table wines that are increasingly up-to-date. We made 7 statements about 7 major Portuguese wine regions. Each statement is in a different letter substitution code – that is **7 different codes** for you to crack. **Do you need an extra help? Each statement uses the word "wine" or "wines" at least once.**

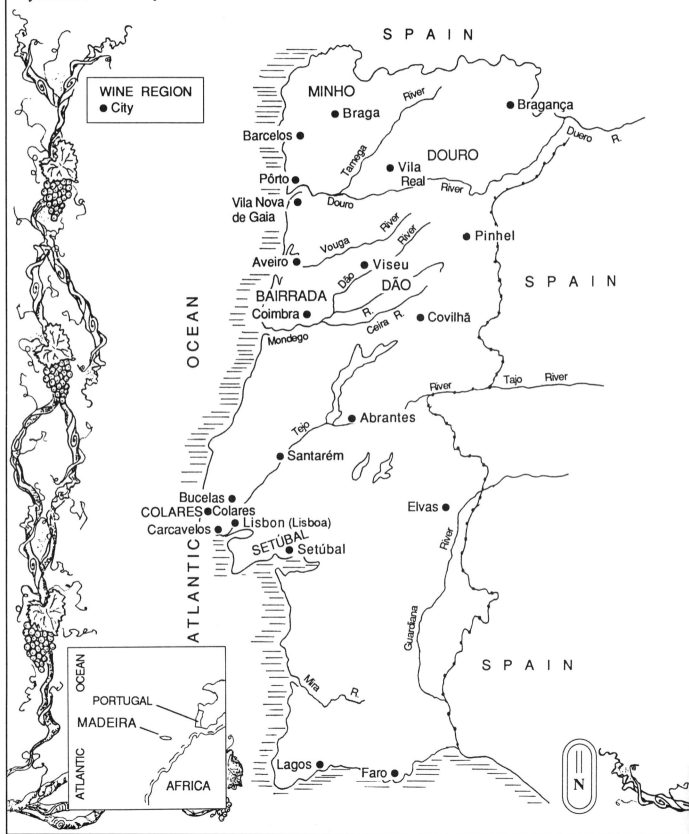

Major Portuguese Wine Regions

1. MINHO ("Vinho Verde" Region):

"KVIIR AMRI?" MX SRPC VIJIVW XS XLI JVIWLRIWW SJ XLIWI AMRIW. XLI ALMXIW OIIT E WPMKLX WTEVOPI.

2. DOURO:

YXAC CNAARCXAH! JWH XO OXACH ANM JWM FQRCN EJARNCRNB LJW KUNWM RWCX BNENAJU BCHUNB XO CQRB OJVXDB OXACRORNM FRWN.

3. DÃO:

BYLY ULY MOVMNUHNCUF LYXM UHX XLS QBCNY QCHYM IZ JLIGCMY.

4. SETÚBAL:

ESP *XZDNLEPW OP DPEFMLW* TD, QCPDS ZC LRPO, L WZGPWJ QZCETQTPO HTYP.

5. COLARES:

AMJYPCQ' PCB *PYKGQAM* EPYNC EPMUQ GL RFC QYLB MD GRQ ZCYAFCQ. JGQZML'Q MRFCP JMAYJ UGLCQ, *AYPAYTCJMQ* YLB *ZSACJYQ*, QSDDCP SPZYL QOSCCXC ML RFCGP TGLCWYPBQ.

6. BAIRRADA:

HVS TWBS KWBSG VSFS, POGSR CB HVS FSR *POUO* UFODS, OUS TCF MSOFG. HVS KVWHS *PWQOZ* UFODS AOYSG GDOFYZWBU KWBSG.

7. MADEIRA:

S MFAIMW TMJFL XDSNGJ AK TSCWV AFLG LZWKW XGJLAXAWV, DGFYWKL- DANWV, DWYWFVSJQ OAFWK.

67. Awakening Aussies

We don't have to "barrack for" the Australian wine industry – the world is already awakening to Australia's wonderful wines. Today, Aussies themselves drink more wine per capita than U.S. citizens. For everyday quaffing, they favor wine sold in cardboard box-dispensers that last for a while. Australia has 4 major winemaking states – New South Wales, Victoria, South Australia, and Western Australia. Each state boasts its own important winegrowing **Locations**. Take a "walkabout" through this timeless land and **identify 9 of those locations (A – I)**. Work back and forth among the **Clues**. We started you off to give you a "fair go."

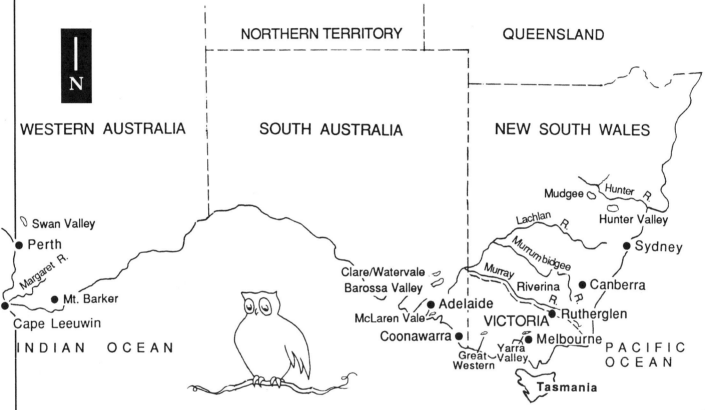

Locations and Clues:

A. **T**his is the capital city of Australia's most productive wine state. It's the home of giant firms such as Seppelt, Penfolds, and Petaluma. To the SE is Location C. Location G is 25 miles NE. Further north, small Clare/Watervale district makes famous fine Rieslings and structured Shiraz,* Cabernet Sauvignon, and Chardonnay. Some of Clare's wineries: Lindemans, Mitchells, Stanley, Grosset, and Enterprise. South of Adelaide is the McLaren Vale territory, with assertive reds, dessert wines, and some Riesling and Chardonnay on its cooler hillsides. Some McLaren wineries are: Coriole, Fern Hill Estate, Thomas Hardy, Wirra Wirra.

A   D   E   L   A   [I / 7]   D   E

B. **A**ustralia has no native vines: the first grape vines were planted in this New South Wales city in 1788. One hundred miles north of this city is Location H. A little farther to the northwest is the cool Mudgee district. Small Mudgee wineries like Huntington Estate produce deep, strong Chardonnay and Cabernet wines.

— — — [/ 6] — —

For more on the Shiraz grape, see Puzzle #68, p. 98.

C. This is Australia's southernmost continental viticulture locale. It's a red-earthed area 250 miles southeast of Location A. Its climate is perfect for Cabernet Sauvignon, Shiraz, Riesling, and Chardonnay. Some wineries here are: Bowen Estate, Brand's Laira, and Lindemans.

— — — — — —|2|— — —

D. This river and the Murrumbidgee River irrigate a region that produces 60+% of Australian grapes. The region includes the Riverina zone in New South Wales and sites in South Australia and in the NW corner of Victoria. Most of the grapes from here go into inexpensive wines. However, in the 1960's, white wine technology led Aussies into serious wine appreciation, so now this large district also raises some finer grapes.

— — — —|5|— — — — — —

E. Western Australia's main wine city. To the NE is warm Swan Valley with its Verdelho, Cabernet Sauvignon, and dessert wines. Wineries are: Olive Farm, Vignacourt, and Sandalford. 200 miles south is the Margaret River domain, the state's quality wine region. It enjoys an ocean influence and is home to the wineries Cape Mentelle, Leeuwin, Moss Wood, Peel Estate, Vasse Felix, and Wrights. To the SE, the new cool, Mount Barker/Frankland precinct specializes in slow-ripening Riesling. Two wineries there: Forest Hill and Plantagenet.

— — —|1|—

F. Capital of the state of Victoria. To the NE, near Rutherglen, is a luscious dessert wine region, with new table wine vineyards in its cooler spots. Some famous producers there are: Brown Bros., Baileys, Morris, Stanton & Killeen. To the west is the Great Western area, home of Seppelt's sparkling wines. The older Yarra Valley blooms again with Riesling, Cabernet Sauvignon, Chardonnay, Pinot Noir, and Gewürztraminer. Some wineries there are: Mount Mary, Seville Estate, Wantirna, Yarra Yering, Yeringberg.

|4|— — — — — — —

G. This is Australia's premier wine valley. Strong reds, famous fortified wines, Sémillon, and Shiraz come from the valley floor. Rieslings are born in the cooler hills. Some notable wineries: Wolf Blass, Henschke, Peter Lehmann, Penfolds, Orlando, Seppelt, Smith's Yalumba.

— — — —|3|— — — — — — —

H. Although its wine leadership passed to South Australia, this hot-summered valley remains important. Its 40+ wineries make smooth Shiraz, plus Sémillon, Cabernet Sauvignon, and Chardonnay. Some respected wineries are: Briar Ridge, Drayton's Bellevue, Lake's Folly, Lindemans, Robson, Rosemount Estate, Rothbury Estate, Tyrrell's Vineyards, and Wyndham Estate.

— — — — — —|8|— — — —

I. **N**ow, write all of the boxed, numbered letters above onto their matching blanks. You will conjure up the name of a promising new, cool Australian area that is even further south than Location C.

— — — — — — I —
1 2 3 4 5 6 7 8

More Australia This Way ⟶

68. Bonzer Aussie Grapes

G'day! Until the 60's, most Australian wines were dessert wines. Then, knowledge of white wine technology and red grape cultivation turned everything around. Australian wines are characterized by interesting grapes, grape names, and grape combinations. Don't be a wowser, mate: get stuck into this. Match these **Aussie Words (1 – 11)** to their **Meanings (A – K)**, and that will also match **Aussie Grapes (1 – 11)** to their **Descriptions (A – K)**.

AUSSIE WORDS

1. BLOKE
2. FLOG
3. BARRACK FOR
4. DINKUM
5. A FAIR GO
6. BONZER
7. GET STUCK INTO
8. SHOUT
9. WOWSER
10. STICKIES
11. PLONK

MEANINGS

A. Very nice
B. Yell encouragement
C. Poor quality wine
D. A good chance
E. Genuine
F. Sell
G. Fellow
H. Puritan; killjoy
I. To treat to a drink
J. Sweet dessert wines
K. To work enthusiastically

GRAPE NAMES

1. CABERNET SAUVIGNON
2. HUNTER RIVER RIESLING
3. SYRAH
4. CHARDONNAY
5. GRENACHE, MERLOT, PINOT NOIR
6. SÉMILLON
7. SULTANA
8. CLARE RIESLING
9. SAUVIGNON BLANC, CHENIN BLANC, GEWÜRZTRAMINER
10. RHINE RIESLING
11. MUSCAT

GRAPE DESCRIPTIONS

A. The Australians bring this grape to mellow perfection: they often blend it with Grape #E.

B. The most widely planted Australian red grape. Aussies re-named this famous French Rhône grape twice - they call it Shiraz and (sometimes) Hermitage. Not at all the same as California's less interesting Petite Sirah, this grape is turned by Australians into a spectrum of desirable styles from light drinkables to thick-fruited, ageable wonders.

C. The base of many celebrated Australian dessert wines.

D. Other popular Aussie reds.

E. Despite their success with Grape #A, Down-Under vintners turned their attention (and many vineyards) over to this more fashionable grape. They often blend it with Grape #A.

F. Aren't they ashamed? In order to flog Sémillon to German settlers, Aussie winemakers renamed it this. Tsk. Tsk.

G. This tannic grape is often softened with Grape #B.

H. Other popular Aussie whites.

I. Aren't they ashamed again? No, just surprised to find that this grape is really the lowly Cruchen Blanc grape. The only similarity it has to the true grape in its name is – whiteness.

J. Unlike Grapes #F and #I, this grape name means what it says.

K. Called "Thompson Seedless" in California, this most-planted grape variety serves as raisins and a base for sparkling wine.

69. Dinkum Facts On Aussie Blends

Add the "E" to each grape, unscramble the letters, and place the resulting words by number on the blanks below.

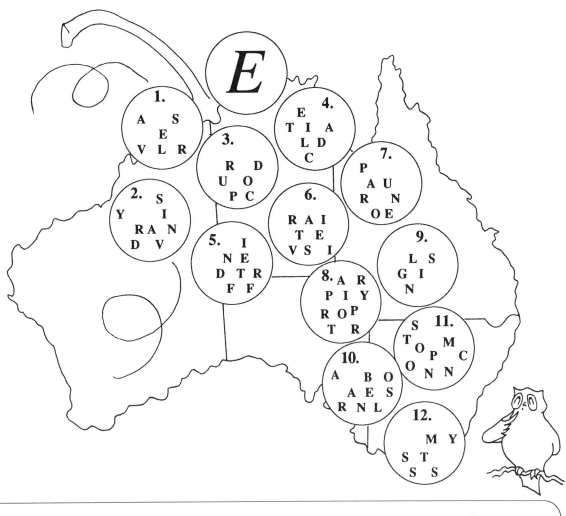

Australian wineries in one region can blend grapes and wines from (1_____ distant regions without saying so on their labels. Many large companies own (2_____ and wineries in separate states and freely blend their (3_____. For example, they strengthen (4_____ wine from Coonawarra with more substantial wine from Clare. Another example is Australian "claret" blended from the red wines of three separate states – New South Wales, Victoria, and South Australia.

Besides blending from (5_____ areas, Aussies blend different (6_____. For instance, they combine Cabernet Sauvignon + Shiraz, Shiraz + Grenache, and Sémillon + Chardonnay.

Aussies give these wines 7_____ names like *Chablis* or *Burgundy*, or (8_____ names like Yarra Yering's *Dry Red #1*. They often state the grape varieties used, but not always their origin. Lately, (9_____ vineyard wines and labeling are becoming popular. So, it seems (10_____ that consumers will eventually get curious about all Australian wines and ask for more specific information about (11_____ and origins. Western Australia and Mudgee in New South Wales are working to develop appellation (12_____ that identify geographic origin. That *is* something new Down Under in the Land of Wonder.

DAFFY DEFINITION: Franconian Bocksbeutel – Not many people care, actually, what this means.

70. Southern Scene

¡Hola! Travel to some important wine areas in South America. Just search our map for locations that fit the clues and the blanks on the opposite page. Remember, we left no spaces to show answers of 2 or more words. (What did you want – super easy?) *¡Buena Suerte!*

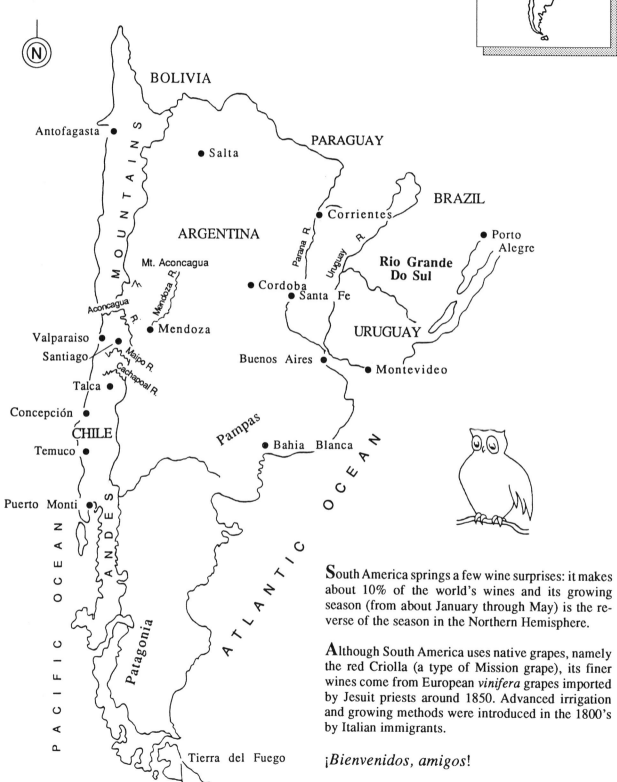

South America springs a few wine surprises: it makes about 10% of the world's wines and its growing season (from about January through May) is the reverse of the season in the Northern Hemisphere.

Although South America uses native grapes, namely the red Criolla (a type of Mission grape), its finer wines come from European *vinifera* grapes imported by Jesuit priests around 1850. Advanced irrigation and growing methods were introduced in the 1800's by Italian immigrants.

¡Bienvenidos, amigos!

1. This country is south America's largest (and the world's 5th largest) winemaker. It drinks most of its own wine and only recently entered the export race. Large conglomerates characterize the wine industry here. Basic red grapes are the native Criolla and the Malbec from Bordeaux; whites are Pedro Ximénes, Palomino, and Torrontes. Cabernet Sauvignon is growing in popularity and finesse, as are Italian Barbera, Nebbiolo, and Sangiovese. Some respected producers are: Peñaflor, Proviar, Suter, and Pascual Toso.

   __ — — — — __ — — —
   2   4

2. This is a state and the main vine region in country #1 (above). A dry, irrigated area, it grows 50% of all South American vines. Its name is the same as a river and a city near Mt. Aconcagua.

   — — — — __ — —
            8

3. This oldest and second-largest South American wine producer makes reds, whites, and sparklers that are considered South America's best. The most favored *vinifera* wines here are Cabernet Sauvignon and Sauvignon Blanc, plus Malbec and Sémillon. These grow in the central valley stretching 160 miles above and below this country's capital city. That capital city is our **Final Answer** below.

   — — __ — —
        5

4. Brazil's southern and major wine state. With a moist, hot climate, this zone relied on native and other non-*vinifera* grapes to make average table fare. Now, especially in this area's southern section, large foreign firms are investing in *vinifera* vineyards.

   — — — __ — — __ — — — — — — — —
         7   3

5. The mountain range between Regions #1 and #3. Its snow provides abundant vineyard water.

   __ — — — __
   6   1

6. **FINAL ANSWER:** Place the numbered letters above onto the matching spaces below and spell the wine-growing capital city of Region #3.

   __ __ __ __ __ __ __ __
   1 2 3 4 5 6 7 8

DAFFY DEFINITION: Chile – cool; the proper way to serve Champagne

71. Chile Challenge

Chalk up cheers for Chile's wines. Our story's **15 CAPITALIZED** words are hiding on the continent below.

Chile's finer wines arise from **TEMPERATE** central districts around **SANTIAGO**. (*See our map on page 100.*) **POLITICS**, and the need for modern cellaring and marketing know-how, keep Chile's wines from having a more dramatic effect on the wine world.

Known especially for **CABERNET** Sauvignon and Sauvignon Blanc wines, Chile is also successful with **MERLOT, RIESLING**, and Sémillon. These classic **VINIFERA** combine with Chile's **VOLCANIC SOIL**, **BORDEAUX**-type growing **METHODS**, new cool white fermentation and red barreling techniques, and geographic protection from *phylloxera* to create world-class **PREMIUM** wines.

Better **WINES** carry "Especial" (barrel-aged 2 years), "**RESERVADO**" (4 years), or "**GRAN VINO**" (6 years) on their labels. Some of Chile's more popular wine producers are: Concha y Toro, Cousiño Macul, Santa Carolina, Santa Rita, Undurraga, Viña Linderos, José Canepa.

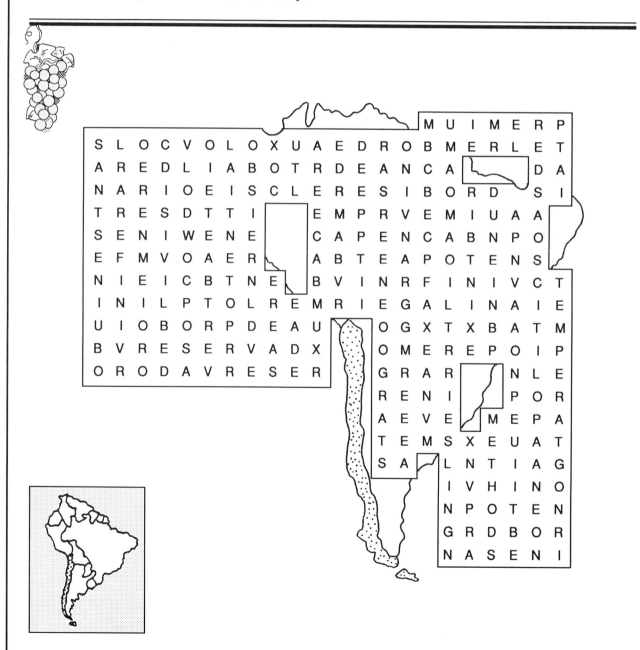

72. There, Too? II

Many more countries than those that we have visited turn grapes into wine. We filled 28 of them into the unique Franconian *bocksbeutel* below. Please serve yourself.

COUNTRIES:

ALGERIA
AUSTRIA
BULGARIA
CANADA
CHINA
CYPRUS
CZECHOSLOVAKIA
EGYPT
ENGLAND
GREECE
HUNGARY
ISRAEL
JAPAN
JORDAN

LEBANON
MEXICO
MOROCCO
NEW ZEALAND
PERU
ROMANIA
SO. AFRICA
SWITZ. (Switzerland)
SYRIA
TUNISIA
TURKEY
UKRAINE
URUGUAY
YUGOSLAVIA

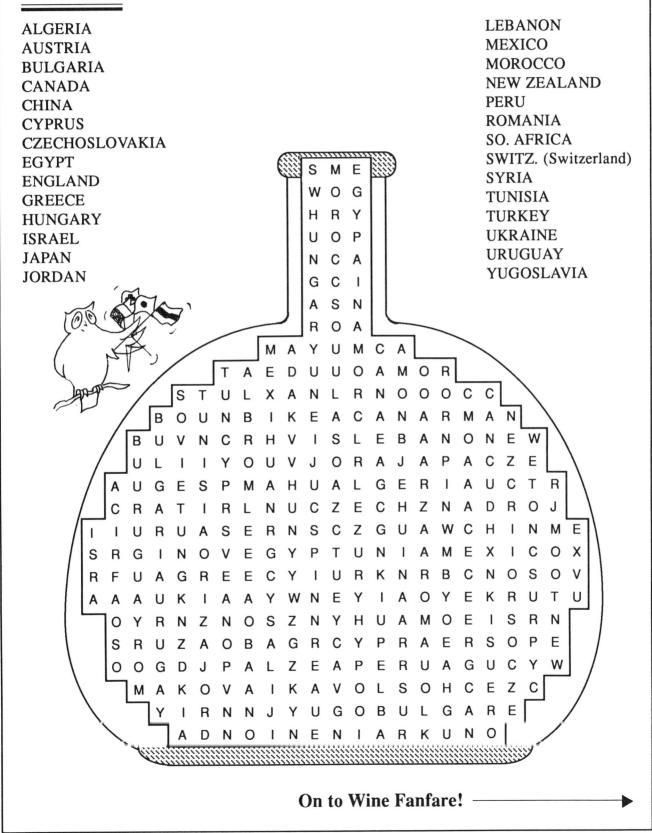

On to Wine Fanfare! ⟶

Welcome to Wine Fanfare!

This is our picnic basket of general wine fun. You solve some of these 28 brain teasers by using wine facts from our preceding **Wine Basics** and **Wine Travels** sections.

73. To Each His Own

"**H**ere," said Fred to 5 of his guests, "are 2 California sparkling wines – a bottle of Hanns Kornell 1987 *Blanc de Noir*, and a magnum of 1983 Schramsberg Reserve."

"Now," said Fred, arranging 6 flute glasses on the table, "I'll bet the Kornell that I can serve one-sixth of the Schramsberg to each of us and still have one-sixth left in the bottle."

"But there are 6 of us," figured one friend. "It can't be done." Fred, however, accomplished what he claimed.

"Well," gloated Fred, pompously opening the Kornell, "I really won this wine for myself, but I'll share my prize. You all can make a toast to my brain power."

"Let's toast your generosity instead," replied one guest dryly.

How did Fred do it?

Whats!?

These designs must be wine phrases. Can you figure them out?

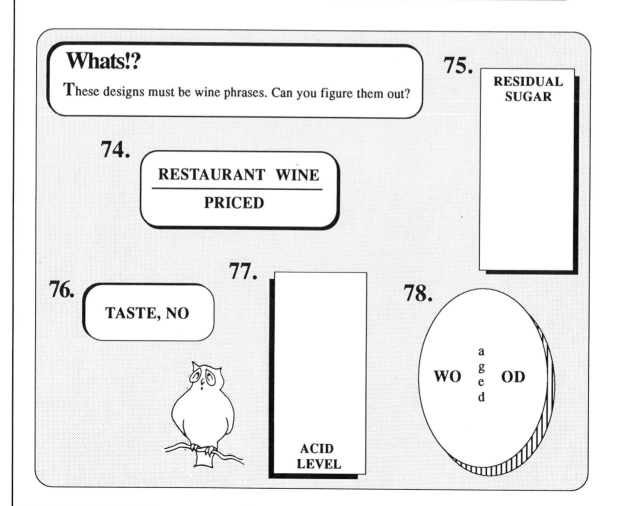

74.

RESTAURANT WINE
———————————
PRICED

75.

RESIDUAL
SUGAR

76.

TASTE, NO

77.

ACID
LEVEL

78.

WO aged OD

79. Bottled Blessing

An old English toast is bottled within. Bubble #1's letters fit vertically into column #1, as you see below. Bubble #2 goes into Column #2, etc. Bottle all the bubbles and read across for our toast.

Besides Grapes

Folks make wine out of a number of interesting things besides grapes. Curious? Decode these substitution codes.

80. One code unlocks all of these 10 items. Here it is: (Quickly! Cover it up if you don't need it.)

If you see:	D	E	F	G	H	I	J	K	L	M	N	O	P	Q	R	S	T	U	V	W	X	Y	Z	A	B	C
It really means:	A	B	C	D	E	F	G	H	I	J	K	L	M	N	O	P	Q	R	S	T	U	V	W	X	Y	Z

1. U L F H
2. S R P H J U D Q D W H V
3. F K H U U L H V
4. U D V S E H U U L H V
5. D S S O H V
6. E O D F N E H U U L H V
7. S O X P V
8. V W U D Z E H U U L H V
9. P L O N
10. S H D F K H V

81. Still curious? Here are 8 more un-grapey* foods that are made into wine. One code breaks all 8 words. We'll tell you that **the code is different from the one in Puzzle #80 above**, but that's all we'll say. Can you still figure out our words?

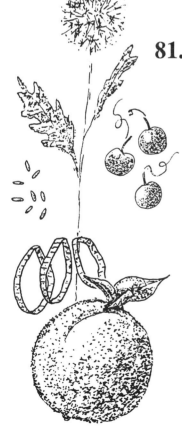

1. B E W Q D R U H H Y U I
2. F U Q H I
3. U B T U H R U H H Y U I
4. S K H H Q D J I
5. S H Q D R U H H Y U I
6. T Q D T U B Y E D I
7. F Y D U Q F F B U I
8. E D Y E D I

*   If it should happen to pop up in conversation, "un-grapey" may also
    be expressed as "non-ampelographic."

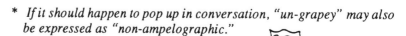

82. He Didn't Like The Water

(Directions are with Puzzle #17 on p. 24.)

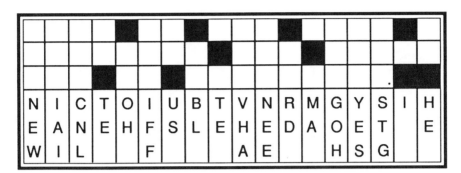

				■			■				■					■	
								■			■						
		■			■									■			
N	I	C		T	O	I	U	B	T	V	N	R	M	G	Y	S	I	H
E	A	N	E	H	F	F	S	L	E	H	E	D	A	O	E	T		E
W	I	L			F					A	E			H	S	G		

Dr. Louis Pasteur

83. Lingering On

Mrs. Murphy is "into" wine. She's informed Mr. Murphy that his cigars prevent her from developing a keener olfactory appreciation of the fruits of the vine. The cigars, indeed *all* smoking, must go.

"But, Darling," Mr. Murphy protested, "I don't indulge in smoking when you taste here, and I certainly never smoke when I wait for you at wine tastings – not since that tasting where they took a vote and threw me out."

"Yes," replied Mrs. M., "but this house and your clothes reek of smoke. It's very impolite to reek at wine tastings."

"Dearest," answered Mr. Murphy piously, "I'll stop smoking forever as soon as I finish this last batch of 27 cigars."

Mrs. Murphy was pleased. "Even if he smokes only one cigar each day," she thought, " that's only 27 more days to wait for unobstructed practice of bouquet exploration."

However, Mr. M. reckoned that if he saved the last third of each cigar and pieced it together with 2 similar butts, he could form another cigar.

If Mr. Murphy smokes one cigar only 2/3 down each day, how long will it be before Mrs. Murphy clears the tasting air?

84. Grape Guess

Long considered a California specialty, this grape forms into a variety of light or deep wines. We cast this mystery grape's name into the pattern below. Can you see it?

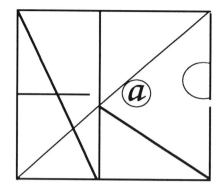

85. So True Of Some Wines

In this code we substituted one letter for another. **Need a hint?** Look below and upside-down.

J X Y I   M Y D U   I X E K B T   R U   U Q J U D –

Y J   Y I   J E E   W E E T   J E   R U   T H K D A.

Jonathan Swift. **Polite Conversation.**

Hint: A really = K, B = L, etc.

86. It's Got "Ine" In It

No, the word "wine" isn't the only wine-related word that contains the letters "ine" in order. Seven other such oenologic nouns lay scrambled below. It will be **fine** if you div**ine** them.

1. ILEARNSM

2. ERYDAVIN

3. NAGREVI

4. CREENAI

5. NEWYIR

6. *RAWZIEMTRENGRÜ*

7. HENIR

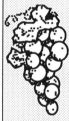

87. Grape Leaf Mix-Up

Each grape leaf grows 6 mixed-up letters. Cultivate some wine words with them. Mix the "T" in Leaf #1 with the letters in Leaf #2, then form those 7 letters into a wine word that answers Definition #2. Mix the same "T" with the letters in Leaf #3, and so on. The boxed letters spell **down** the answer to Definition #1.

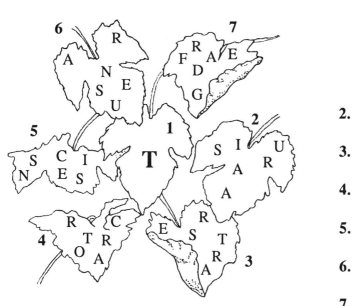

1.

T

2. _ _ _ _ _ _ _

3. _ _ _ _ _ _ _

4. _ _ _ _ _ _ _

5. _ _ _ _ _ _ _

6. _ _ _ _ _ _ , _

7. _ _ _ _ _ _ _

Definitions

1. Wine tryout.
2. A wine-loving country SE of Germany.
3. General name for any strong yeast culture that is used to begin fermentation.
4. Soil preparing vehicle.
5. Vine enemies (i.e., leafhoppers, aphids).
6. Chaptalization, or wine sugaring, is not Mother _____'_ own sweet way.
7. One *phylloxera* solution is: European vines _____ onto American root stock.

88. Stand By Your Wine

Wines go in and out of fashion so quickly: if you fearlessly stick to the styles you like – they'll eventually catch on again. **For example**, red...

Puzzle directions are with Puzzle #17, p. 24

Whats!? II

Remember the **Whats!?** (Puzzles #74 – 78)? How about a second helping?

89.

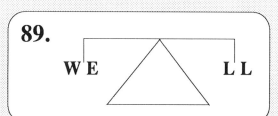

90.

91. ffffiiiinnnnniiiisssshhhh

92.

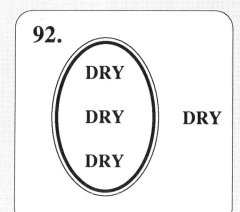

93. Minus And Plus

Try your hand at blending! Below is a list of paired words. Take one letter from the first word and blend it into the second word. Unscramble the letters left in the first word, then unscramble the letters in the second word. You'll create 2 related wine words. **Example: nuns** and **air** = **sun** and **rain**

1. **riven** and **pages** = _____ and _____

2. **stance** and **test** = _____ and _____

3. **rides** and **whets** = _____ and _____

4. **toils** and **wear** = _____ and _____

5. **messed** and **sets** = _____ and _____

6. **dyer** and **west** = _____ and _____

94. The Wine Amigos

Ready for a little logic? We give you clues; you consider them in relation to each other and use the grid to mark down your conclusions. Think deeply and sample the lives of some active California wine consumers.

Five Los Angeles couples attend California wine events together. The ladies are: **Alice**, **Betty**, **Carol**, **Dierdre**, and **Enid**. Their husbands (alphabetically) are: Misters **Adair**, **Green**, **Lenitch**, **Onawa**, and **Sanchez**. At a recent tasting, each couple chose a different California wine to add to its list of favorites. The wines were: a **Cabernet Sauvignon** (Heitz Cellars, Martha's Vineyard '87), a **Chardonnay** (Clos Du Bois, Alexander Valley '90), a **Fumé Blanc** (Konocti Cellars Estate '89), a **Johannisberg Riesling** (Jekel Vineyards Monterey '90), and a **Zinfandel** (Kenwood, Jack London Vineyard '90).

Search the following clues, draw the right conclusions, mark them down on the grid, and match each lady to her man and each wine to the couple who liked it best. (Clue 2 tells us that neither the Adairs nor the Greens chose the Riesling. We marked the grid to show that.)

CLUES

1. Three years ago, Alice and the Fumé lover's wife attended a Napa Valley wine appreciation course. There they met Mr. and Mrs. Adair and the Zin chooser's wife.
2. The Adairs, Greens, and the Riesling couple recently enjoyed a vertical* tasting of Papagni Vineyards' *Alicante Bouschet* ('80, '84, '88) and Joseph Phelps' *Insignia* blend ('82, '83, '84, '85, '86, '87).
3. The Cabernet was the Adair's second choice.
4. Betty and her husband first met the others a year ago at the *Wine Spectator* Scholarship tasting.
5. Betty and Mrs. Onawa know a wine shop owner who invited them to special tastings for retailers. These tastings were held June 2 – 5 in San Francisco.
6. Mr. Onawa's wife and Carol bought surprises for their spouses. A Sonoma vineyard "sold" them each a 15-year "ownership" of one of its producing Pinot Noir vines.
7. Mrs. Sanchez used the first week of June to tour the small, active Santa Cruz wineries with the Riesling wife.
8. Mr. Onawa, the Zin couple, and Dierdre and her husband plan a wine tasting-hot air balloon trip in Napa.

* A vertical tasting is a sampling and comparing of different vintages or years of the same kind of wine from the same winery.

DAFFY DEFINITION: Vertical Tasting – one where tasters control themselves and do not need to assume a horizontal position.

Whats!? III

Trust us. We promise that this is the last of them.

95.

96.

AIЯƎT

97.

G bOtTL

98.

E D R , WINES

99. Ten-Fours

Ten four-letter wine words hide in these 15 letters. You've met all 10 words already, so you should easily uncover them. Our puzzle design is inspired by the practice of night grape harvesting. In California, bringing in grapes between 10 p.m. and 7:00 a.m. keeps them cool and maintains high fruit quality before crushing.

K E D I C
T S O R T
L I P N U

1. Season's harvest — **CROP**
2. "Strength" mineral in grapes — _____
3. "Over the _____, between the gums..." — _____
4. Restaurant's wine roster — _____
5. "Black" in France; Pinot ____ — _____
6. A wine's general nasal appeal — _____
7. Fortified wine of Portugal made in California's Central Valley — _____
8. "Sparkling" wine in Germany — _____
9. Earth home for vines — _____
10. Too much oxygen can _____ wine into vinegar. — _____

100. There Is A Season

Winemaking activities overlap from month to month, depending on area, weather, etc. Yet, some months seem to be traditionally associated with certain wine tasks and events. See if you can match the **Month** to the **Wine Task Or Event** usually connected with it.

Each **Clue** below suggests a certain month of the year. The answer to **Clue A.** – *Bustin' out all over* – is **June**, so we wrote "June" on the blank that follows Clue A. Now we can see that June is the traditional month when the vine flowers and pollinates and when berries form, or "set." Do the same with every Clue and soon you'll match every Month to its Wine Task Or Event.

Jan. Feb. Mar. Apr. May June July Aug. Sept. Oct. Nov. Dec.

CLUES	MONTH	WINE TASK OR EVENT
A. Bustin' out all over	JUNE	Vine flowers and pollinates; berries form, or "set"
B. ...as molasses in...	_____	Continue pruning; bottle mature wines
C. Scary	_____	Harvest and crush continues
D. ...Of The Toy Soldiers	_____	Cultivate earth; weed; vines start to sprout canes
E. Shortest month	_____	Rack new wines
F. A May/_____ marriage	_____	Prune; test new wines; start to bottle mature ones
G. _____ Song	_____	Harvest and crush
H. _____ Showers	_____	Clean vineyard; plant new vines
I. Last of summer	_____	Red (black) grapes turn dark; prepare machines and vats for harvest
J. Dec...	_____	Continue to spray* vines; berries are small and green
K. _____	_____	Look out for frost; cut ground suckers; fruit buds appear; fight weeds; spray* for mildew
L. _____	_____	Harvest ending; prepare soil and vines for winter; prepare to bottle mature wines

Keep in mind Puzzle #52 on organic winegrowing: certain traditional practices are being re-thought or abandoned.

Important...

Wine in moderation is enjoyed by thousands, and its health benefits are sung by many doctors and experts, but, as with any food, wine still might not be right for you as an individual and all the praises in the world won't make it so. Ask at your library and doctor's about wine and alcohol, especially in relation to allergies and to pregnancy. The author and publisher urge you, our reader, to make an informed decision about yourself and all alcoholic beverages.

Answers –
Just around this corner

Thanks for playing along with us!

ANSWERS

1.

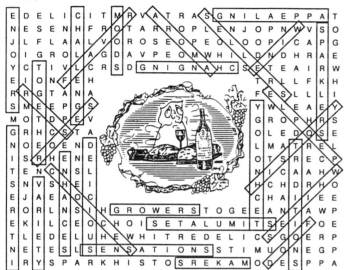

2. fortified

3. table

4. sparkling

5. aperitif

6. dessert

7. 1. blend   2. expect   3. foods
     4. enjoyable   5. order   6. filet

8. 1. knight   2. scary   3. plow
     4. venom   5. feud   6. box

Its label may state only one grape type, but
the wine can contain a percentage of other
grape varieties. Even with other grapes
added to it, a good varietal expresses the best
qualities of the grape listed on the label.

9.

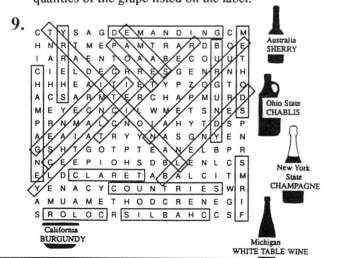

10.

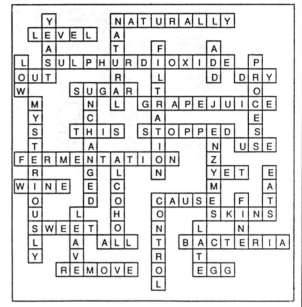

11.

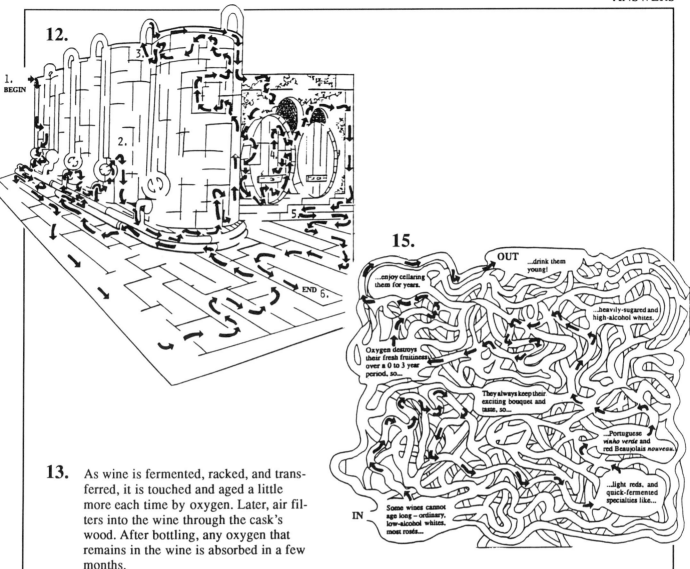

12.

1.
BEGIN

15.

OUT

...drink them young!

...enjoy cellaring them for years.

...heavily-sugared and high-alcohol whites.

Oxygen destroys their fresh fruitiness over a 0 to 3 year period, so...

They always keep their exciting bouquet and taste, so...

...Portuguese *vinho verde* and red Beaujolais *nouveau.*

...light reds, and quick-fermented specialties like...

IN

Some wines cannot age long – ordinary, low-alcohol whites, most rosés...

13. As wine is fermented, racked, and transferred, it is touched and aged a little more each time by oxygen. Later, air filters into the wine through the cask's wood. After bottling, any oxygen that remains in the wine is absorbed in a few months.

14. If a wine is full of alcohol, tannin, sugar, acid, or other strong ingredients, it needs time to blend, soften, and become a many-splendored thing. Wine lovers "lay down" such wines for years (and decades) until this marriage happens. Then, owners drink these wines before oxygen overmatures and spoils them. Examples: reds – fine clarets, burgundies, and port; whites – Sauternes, the best German Rieslings, and burgundies.

15 Continued

The useful phrases read:
Some wines cannot age long – ordinary, low-alcohol whites, most rosés, light reds, and quick-fermented specialties like Portuguese *vinho verde* and red Beaujolais *nouveau.* Oxygen destroys their fresh fruitiness over a 0 to 3 year period, so, drink them young!

16. A. Slow oxidation also enhances the bouquet of the wine.
B. Oxidation helps a wine's alcohol and fruit acid to combine.
C. This creates esters (compounds) which give off lovely aromas.

17. ...if the cork dries and shrinks, then too much oxygen will rush in and ruin the wine.

18. Read the sentences in this order: 8, 12, 3, 10, 6, 2, 1, 11, 4, 9, 7, 5.

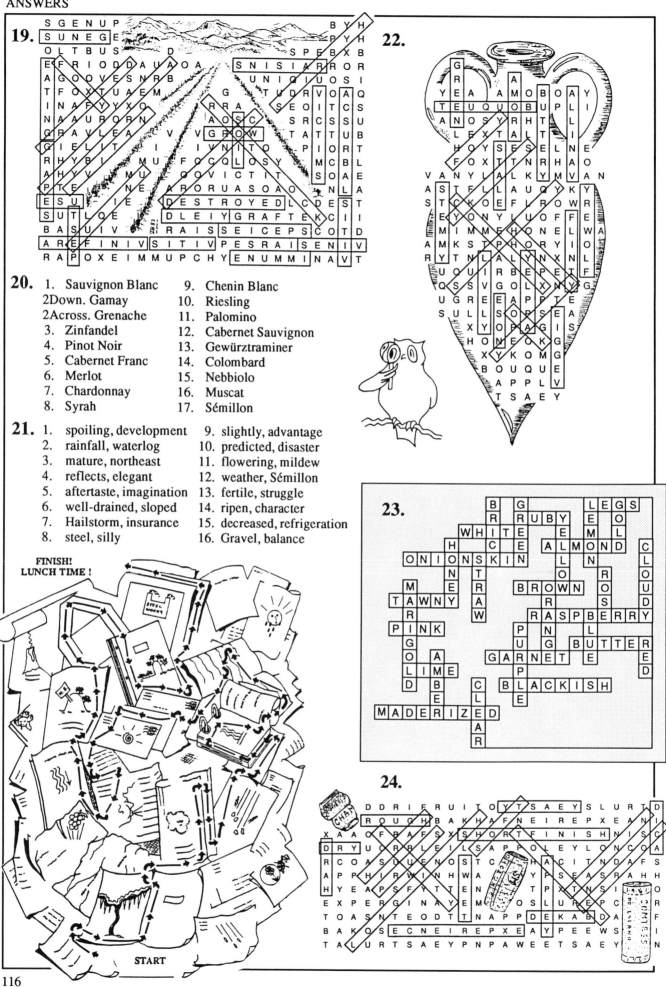

19.

20.

1. Sauvignon Blanc	9. Chenin Blanc
2Down. Gamay	10. Riesling
2Across. Grenache	11. Palomino
3. Zinfandel	12. Cabernet Sauvignon
4. Pinot Noir	13. Gewürztraminer
5. Cabernet Franc	14. Colombard
6. Merlot	15. Nebbiolo
7. Chardonnay	16. Muscat
8. Syrah	17. Sémillon

21.

1. spoiling, development	9. slightly, advantage
2. rainfall, waterlog	10. predicted, disaster
3. mature, northeast	11. flowering, mildew
4. reflects, elegant	12. weather, Sémillon
5. aftertaste, imagination	13. fertile, struggle
6. well-drained, sloped	14. ripen, character
7. Hailstorm, insurance	15. decreased, refrigeration
8. steel, silly	16. Gravel, balance

22.

23.

24.

FINISH!
LUNCH TIME !

START

25.

1 = G.	Traditional port	6 = H. Long-necked port
2 = C.	Champagne bottle	7 = B. Chianti *fiasco*
3 = F.	Rhine	8 = A. Bordeaux
4 = E.	Half-liter	9 = D. Champagne magnum
5 = I.	Franconian *bocksbeutel*	10 = J. Burgundy

26.

1 = A.	Basic clear	6 = D. Anjou
2 = E.	Hock	7 = G. Engraved Mosel
3 = B.	Cognac	8 = I. Taster's glass
4 = C.	Alsace	9 = H. Sparkling wine/ Champagne
5 = F.	Sherry *copita*	

27.

28.

29.

30.

31. Dry wines before sweet; young before old; white wines before red; and least wines before best.

32. "This is the beautiful thing about wine: you make up your own rules."   Joe Heitz

33.

34.

LSOUDH = should
SLIPGENA = pleasing
GREVNIA = vinegar
SUHMY = mushy
SNOONI = onions
SCRITU = citrus
HSLAC = clash
PONSITXEEC = exceptions
ETWES = sweet
HILTG = light
SECKOIO = cookies
UMSAOF = famous
THASIB = habits
CIE BECSU = ice cubes
JYONE = enjoy
PILSEM = simple
VIPEXNEES = expensive
AHPEC = cheap
SLEETT = settle
IFEMETIL = lifetime
USLAPERE = pleasure
OG ROF TI = Go for it!

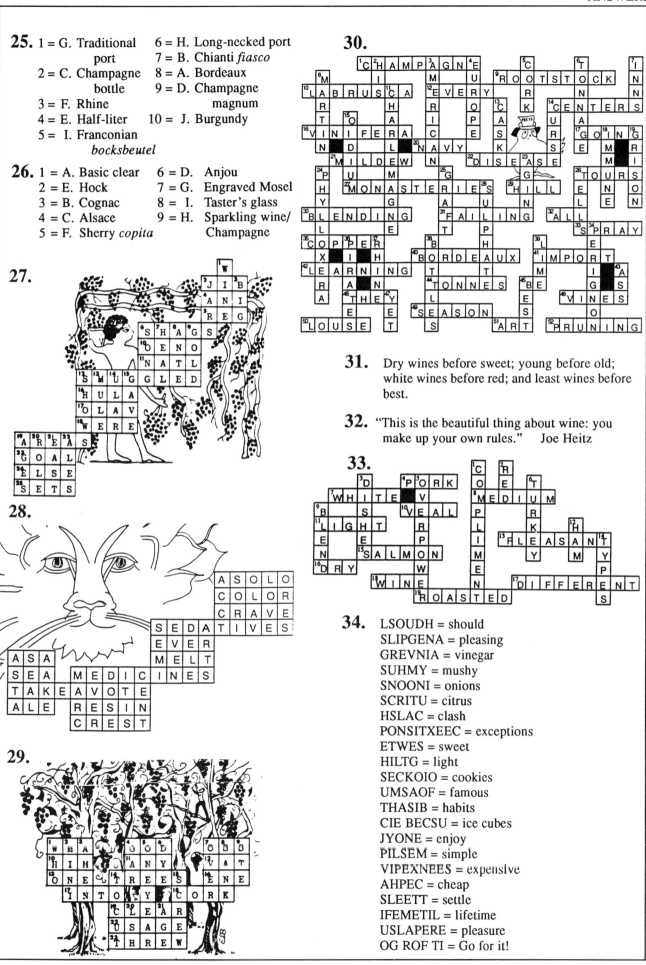

117

34. Con't.

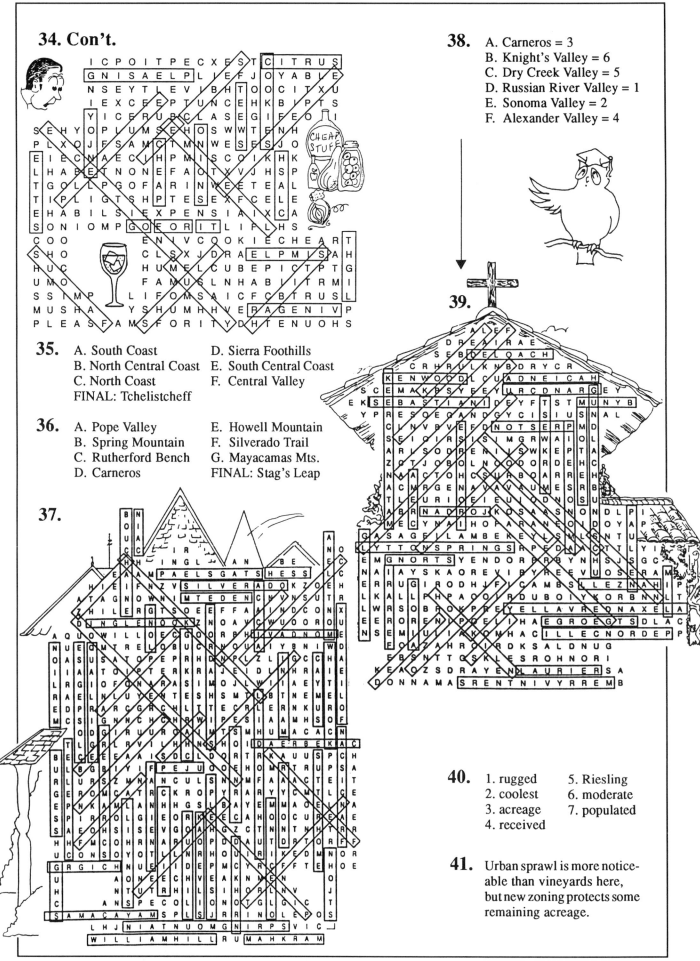

35.
A. South Coast
B. North Central Coast
C. North Coast
D. Sierra Foothills
E. South Central Coast
F. Central Valley
FINAL: Tchelistcheff

36.
A. Pope Valley
B. Spring Mountain
C. Rutherford Bench
D. Carneros
E. Howell Mountain
F. Silverado Trail
G. Mayacamas Mts.
FINAL: Stag's Leap

37.

38.
A. Carneros = 3
B. Knight's Valley = 6
C. Dry Creek Valley = 5
D. Russian River Valley = 1
E. Sonoma Valley = 2
F. Alexander Valley = 4

39.

40.
1. rugged
2. coolest
3. acreage
4. received
5. Riesling
6. moderate
7. populated

41. Urban sprawl is more noticeable than vineyards here, but new zoning protects some remaining acreage.

42.

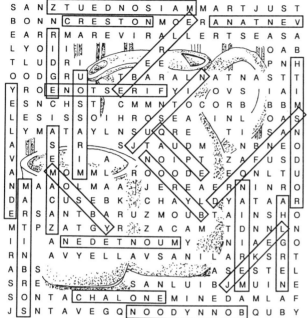

46.

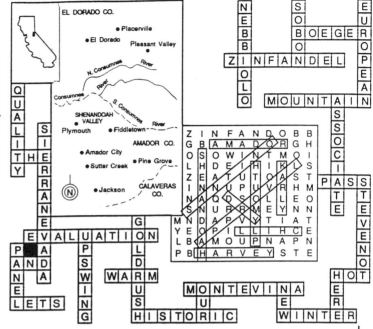

43. Felicia and Ann didn't phone or interview (Clue 2). Steve didn't interview (Clue 2), so he phoned. Adoni interviewed the wine shop owner. The wine shop owner told Adoni about technical progress in the Central Valley (Clue 4), and Steve got the grape information (Clue 5). Ann found no geographical data (Clue 6), so she learned about big wineries and Felicia found geographical info. Ann used the library, but not the book (Clue 6). Felicia used the book, and Ann used the magazine article.

44. For **generations**, the Ficklin family of Madera has planted **genuine** Portuguese grapes and **fashioned** them into **respected** port **wines**. The **newer** port **maker** in the area, Quady, also **creates popular dessert** wines from Muscat **grapes**.

45. ...islands, houseboats, historic inns, rich soil, warm days, and cool mornings and evenings.

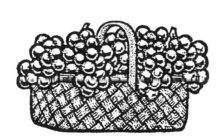

47.

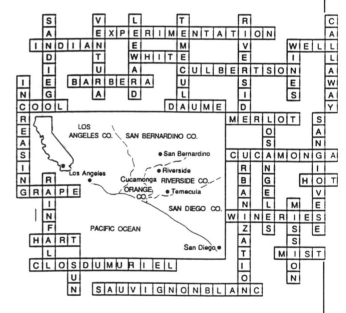

48. ...ideas are first laughed at, then secretly tried, and then often quickly adopted.

49. Lucky, boast, unique, different, other, winemakers, favorite, make some, distinctive, example, move, away, power, subtle.

50. Many blended wines still use ordinary grapes, for example, the Thompson Seedless, as their base. However, the new trend is to blend several noble varieties together into premium wines. For instance, numerous California wineries make blends as they do in Bordeaux. They've given these Bordeaux styles a collective name – *Meritage*. Other California wineries grow and combine grapes used in the French Rhône region, such as Grenache, Mourvèdre, and Syrah, into delicious table wines and aperitifs. To create the most pleasing tastes, winemakers mix grapes as they like and even blend finished wines from different countries.

51. Each picture or letter/word in order = California, tacked, wines, grape, but (butt, or wine cask), tied, could (C + hood), well, vineyards, California, masters (mast + ers), to, soils (s + oil + s), for example (4 X + M + pill), to, Californians, are (R), seeing, start (star + T), years, that (T + hat), and (hand – H), varieties (Vr + eye + ah + T's).

52. 1. dioxide 2. destroying 3. Organic 4. pesticide 5. unfiltered 6. specialize 7. bubblies 8. complexity

53. 1 = X   2 = K   3 = A, G, Q, Y   4 = O   5 = I   6 = S   7 = B, E, T   8 = R   9 = W
10 = F, M   11 = J   12 = U, V, AA, BB   13 = N   14 = L, Z   15 = C   16 = D, H   17 = P

54. ...musical chairs – changing jobs and launching their own consulting firms and wineries.

55.

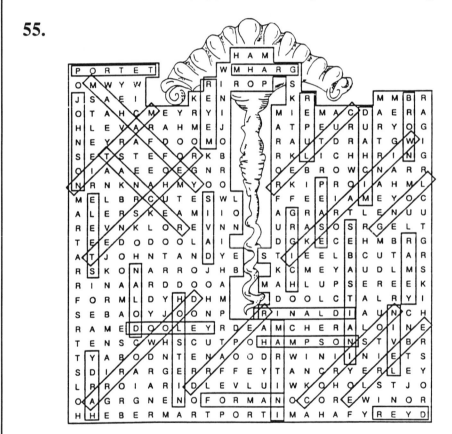

56. 1 = E, 2 = I, 3 = G, 4 = A, 5 = H, 6 = F, 7 = C, 8 = B, 9 = D

57. 1 = I, 2 = H, 3 = G, 4 = E, 5 = B, 6 = K, 7 = C, 8 = J, 9 = A, 10 = F, 11 = D

58. 1. Seattle 2. trucked 3. Yakima 4. hilly 5. traditions 6. Portland 7. western 8. wineries

59. I. Read the sentences in this order: 6, 3, 9, 1, 7, 10, 2, 5, 8, 11, 4

II. Read the sentences in this order: 5, 1, 7, 2, 8, 6, 3, 9, 4.

III. Read the sentences in this order: 6, 2, 4, 3, 7, 8, 1, 5.

IV. Read the sentences in this order: 5, 8, 3, 2, 7, 4, 6, 9, 1, 10

60. **Area #1** = Lake Erie, **Area #2** = Long Island, **Area #3** = Finger Lakes, **Area #4** = Hudson River Valley

61.

62. Region #1 = Alsace   2 = Rhône   3 = Bordeaux   4 = Marseille   5 = Provence (We hope that you didn't fit in the name of the Bordeaux town of Pauillac. Pauillac is one of the world's worshipped wine shrines and is not near Toulon.)   6 = Saône   7 = Languedoc   8 = Burgundy   9 = Loire · FINAL = Champagne

63. A. Rheinpfalz = 3   B. Franken = 6   C. Baden = 1   D. Nahe = 4   E. Württemberg = 2
F. Rheinhessen = 5   G. Mittelrhein = 9   H. Mosel-Saar-Ruwer = 7   I. Rheingau = 8   J. Ahr = 10

64. Region #1 = Piedmont   2 = Trentino-Alto Adige   3 = Veneto   4 = Friuli-Venezia-Giulia   5 = Emilia-Romagna   6 = Tuscany   7 = Lombardy   8 = Latium   9 = Campania   10 = Apulia   11 = Sicily   12 = Sardinia

65. A = 5, B = 8, C = 6, D = 9, E = 7, F = 1, G = 2, H = 3, I = 4

66. **1. (In this first code, A = W) Minho (Vinho Verde region):** "Green wine?" It only refers to the freshness of these wines. The whites keep a slight sparkle.   **2. (A = R) Douro:** Port territory! Any of forty red and white varieties can blend into several styles of this famous fortified wine.   **3. (A = G) Dão:** Here are substantial reds and dry white wines of promise.   **4. (A = L) Setúbal:** The *Moscatel de Setúbal* is, fresh or aged, a lovely fortified wine.   **5. (A = C) Colares:** Colares' red *Ramisco* grape grows in the sand of its beaches. Lisbon's other local wines, *Carcavelos* and *Bucelas*, suffer urban squeeze on their vineyards.   **6. (A = M) Bairrada :** The fine wines here, based on the red *Baga* grape, age for years. The white *Bical* grape makes sparkling wines.   **7. (A = I) Madeira:** A unique burnt flavor is baked into these fortified, longest-lived, legendary wines.

67.   1 = Adelaide   6 = Melbourne
2 = Sydney   7 = Barossa Valley
3 = Coonawarra   8 = Hunter Valley
4 = Murray River   FINAL: Tasmania
5 = Perth

68. 1 = G 2 = F 3 = B 4 = E 5 = D 6 = A
7 = K 8 = I 9 = H 10 = J 11 = C

69. 1 = several 2 = vineyards 3 = produce
4 = delicate 5 = different 6 = varieties
7 = European 8 = proprietary 9 = single
10 = reasonable 11 = components 12 = systems

70. 1 = Argentina 2 = Mendoza 3 = Chile 4 = Rio
Grande Do Sul 5 = Andes FINAL: Santiago

71.

72.

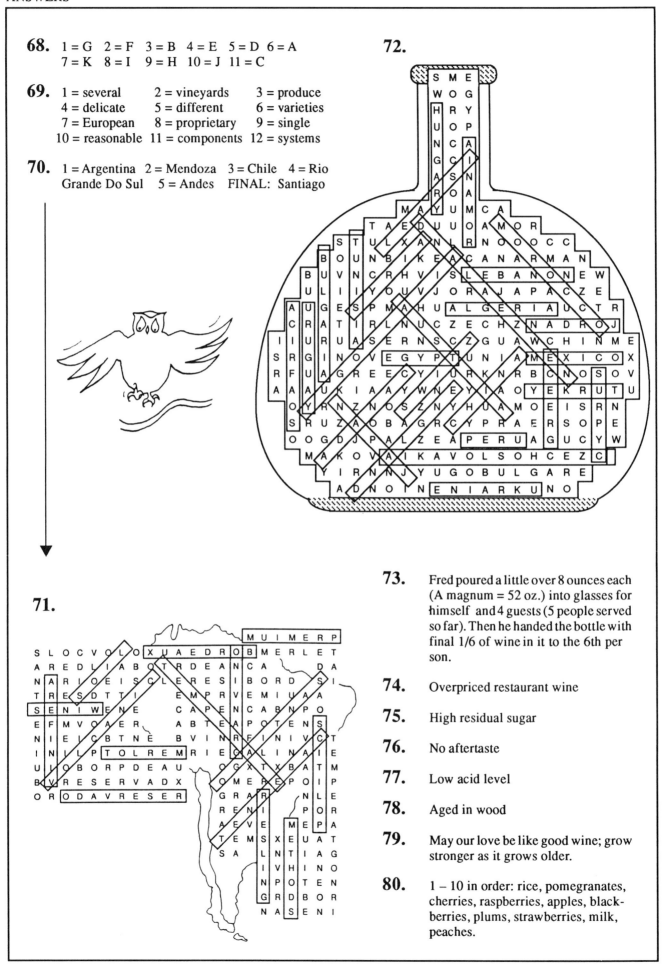

73. Fred poured a little over 8 ounces each (A magnum = 52 oz.) into glasses for himself and 4 guests (5 people served so far). Then he handed the bottle with final 1/6 of wine in it to the 6th person.

74. Overpriced restaurant wine

75. High residual sugar

76. No aftertaste

77. Low acid level

78. Aged in wood

79. May our love be like good wine; grow stronger as it grows older.

80. 1 – 10 in order: rice, pomegranates, cherries, raspberries, apples, blackberries, plums, strawberries, milk, peaches.

81. (In this code, the letter A = K) 1 – 10 in order: loganberries, pears, elderberries, currants, cranberries, dandelions, pineapples, onions

82. "Wine is the most healthful and hygienic of beverages."

83. 27 cigars (smoked 2/3 down) = 27 ends
27 ends ÷ 3 = 9 more cigars (smoked 2/3 down) = 9 ends
9 ends ÷ 3 = 3 more cigars (smoked 2/3 down) = 3 ends
3 ends ÷ 3 = 1 cigar
27 + 9 + 3 + 1 = 40 cigars = 40 days

84. Zinfandel

85. "This wine should be eaten – it is too good to be drunk."

86. 1. minerals   2. vineyard   3. vinegar   4. cinerea   5. winery   6. Gewürztraminer   7. Rhine

87. 1 = tasting   2 = Austria   3 = starter   4 = tractor   5 = insects   6 = Nature's   7 = grafted

88. (red)...Zinfandel was "in" ten years ago; then, white Zin and "blush" were the rage. Now, red Zins are regaining respect.

89. Well-balanced

90. Noble rot

91. Long finish

92. Extra dry

93. 1. vine and grapes   2. scent and taste   3. reds and whites   4. soil and water   5. seeds and stems
6. dry and sweet

94. The Adairs are not the Fumé or Zin couple (Clue 1), Riesling (Clue 2), nor Cab lovers (Clue 3). The Adairs pick Chardonnay. The Riesling is not first with the Adairs, Greens (Clue 2), the Onawas (Clues 5 and 7), or the Sanchez' (Clue 7). Lenitch takes Riesling. Betty's wine is not Riesling (Clues 5 and 7), Chard (the Adairs'), Fumé, or Zin (Clues 1 and 4). Betty chooses Cabernet. Alice's wine is not Zin or Fumé (Clue 1), Chard (Clue 1 – Alice is not Mrs. Adair), nor Cab (Betty's). Alice picks Riesling and is Mrs. Lenitch. Betty's Cabernet spouse is not Sanchez or Onawa (Clues 5 and 7), Adair (Chard), or Lenitch (Alice). Betty is Mrs. Green. Mr. Onawa doesn't opt for Chard (Adair), Riesling (Lenitch), Cab (Green), or Zin (Clue 8). He likes Fumé Blanc. Mr. Sanchez likes what's left – Zinfandel. Mrs. Onawa is not Carol (Clue 6), Dierdre (Clue 8), Betty, or Alice. Enid is Mrs. Onawa. Mrs. Sanchez is not Dierdre (Clue 8), Enid, Alice, or Betty. Carol is Mrs. Sanchez, so Dierdre is Mrs. Adair.

95. Fruity (Fruit E)   **96.** Bacteria   **97.** Bottling (Bottl in G)   **98.** After dinner wines (D in ER)

99. 1. crop   2. iron   3. lips   4. list   5. noir   6. nose   7. port   8. sekt   9. soil   10. turn

100.
A = June
B = Jan.
C = Oct.
D = Mar.
E = Feb.
F = Dec.
G = Sept.
H = Apr.
I = Aug.
J = July
K = May
L = Nov.

Pronouncing Guide

oh = long o sound as in "only"
zh = the sound of z in "azure"

Aconcagua	ah-kohn-KAH-gwa	Dão	DAH-oh
Ahr	ahr	Dijon	dee-zhohn
Airén	eye-RAYN	Dionysus	dye-uh-NYE-suss
Alicante Bouschet	ah-lee-KAHN-tay boo-SHAY	Dom Pérignon	dawm pay-reen-yawn
Alsace	ahl-zahss	Douro	doo-roh
amphora (ae)	AM-fah-rah (eye)		
Anjou	awn-zhoo	Emilia-Romagna	eh-MEEL-yah roh-MAHN-yah
aperitif	ah-pair-ee-TEEF	enology	ee-NOLL-uh-jee
Apulia	ah-POOL-yah	especial	A-spay-see-AHL
Asti Spumante	AH-stee spoo-MAHN-teh		
		fiasco (fiaschi)	fee-AHS-koh (fee-AHS-kee)
Bacchus	BACK-uss	filet	fih-LAY
Bad Kreuznach	bahd KROYTZ-nakh	Folie à Deux	foh-lee ah dew
Bad Münster	bahd MEWN T-ster	Franken	FRAHN-ken
Bairrada	bye-RAH-dah	Friuli-Venezia-	free-OO-lee veh-NET-zee-ah
Barbaresco	bahr-bah-RESS-coh	Giulia	JOO-lee-ah
Barbera	bar-BAIR-ah	Fumé	foo-MAY
Bastei	bahs-TIE		
Barolo	ba-ROH-loh	Gamay	gam-may
Beaujolais nouveau	boh-zho-LAY noo-voh	generic	jen-AIR-ik
Beaulieu	bowl-YUH	Gewürztraminer	geh-VERTZ-trah-mee-ner
Bernkastel	BAIRN-castl	Goldtröpfchen	gold-truhpf-shehn
blanc	blahn	Gran Vino	grahn VEE-noh
bocksbeutel	BAWKS-boydl	Grenache	greh-NAHSH
Bordeaux	bore-doh	Grgich	GUR-gitch
botrytis cinerea	bo-TRY-tiss sin-EH-ray-ah	Gundlach-Bundschu	gunn-lockh-bunn-shoe
Bourgogne	boor-GON-yuh		
Brix	bricks	Healdsburg	HEELDS-berg
		Heitz (Joe)	hights
Cabernet Sauvignon	kah-bair-NAY so-veen-yohn	Hermitage	air-mee-tahj
Cabernet Franc	kah-bair-NAY frahn		
Canandaigua	kan-nan-DAY-gwah	Jerez de la Frontera	hair-AITH day lah
carafe	kah-RAFF or kah-RAHF		frohn-TAY-rah
Carcavelos	car-cah-VAY-lohss	Johannisberg Riesling	yo-HAHN-iss-bairg REES-ling
Carneros	car-NAIR-ohss		
Chablis	shah-blee	Kahlenberg	kah-lehn-bairg
Chappellet	shah-peh-LAY	Konocti	kuh-NOCK-tee
Champagne	sham-PAIN		
chaptalize	SHAHP-tah-lize	labrusca	lah-BRUCE-kah
Chardonnay	shar-doh-NAY	Languedoc	lahn-guh-doc
Château De Baun	shah-toh duh bone	Léon Millot	lay-ohn mee-oh
Château Grillet	shah-toh gree-yay	Loire	lwahr
Château Pétrus	shah-toh peh-troos	Louis Vuitton	loo-ee vwee-tawn
Château Souverain	shah-toh soo-veh-RAIN	Lyon	lee-awn
Châteauneuf-du-Pape	shah-toh-nuf-doo-pahp		
Chelois	shell-oy	Madeira	mah-DEAR-uh
Chenin Blanc	sheh-nan blahn		(Spanish = mah-DAY-rah)
Chianti	key-AHN-tee	Main (River)	mine
claret	CLAIR-et	Maison Deutz	may-zawn ("Deutz" sounds like
Clos du Bois	cloh duh BWAH		"puts" as in "puts it down."
Clos Pegase	cloh peh-GAHSS	Málaga	MAH-lah-gah
cognac	kone-yak, also kahn-yak	Malvasia	mahl-VAH-see-ah
Colares	coo-LAH-rayss	Marche	MAR-kay
copita	koh-PEE-tah	Maréchal Foch	mah-reh-shal fawsh
Côte Rôtie	coat roh-tee	Marne	mahrn

Marseille	mar-say	Riesling	REESE-ling
Mayacamas	my-yah-KAHM-ahss	Rio Grande do Sul	REE-oh GRAHN-day duh
Merlot	mair-loh		sool
methyl	meh-thl an-thran-EYE-late	Rioja	ree-OH-ha
anthranilate	*also* an-THRAN-ih-late	Riunite	ree-oo-NEE-tee
Midi	mee-dee	Roederer	ROH-der-er
Minho	MEEN-yoh	rosé	roh-ZAY
Mirassou	meer-ah-soo	Rueda	roo-A-dah
Mittelrhein	MITT'L-rine		
Moët & Chandon	mo-ET eh chawn-dawn	saccharomyces	sack-uh-ro-MY-seez
Montilla-Moriles	mohn-TEEL-yah	Sangiovese	sahn-jo-VAY-zeh
	moh-REE-layss	Santa Ynez	SAHN-tie ee-NAYSS
Moscato *(Italian spell.*		Santiago	sahn-tee-AH-go
of Muscat)	mohss-CAH-toh	Saumur	saw-mur
Mosel *(Germ. spelling)*	MO-zl	Sauternes	saw-tairn
Mosel-Saar-Ruwer	MO-zl-sahr-ROO-ver	Sauvignon Blanc	soh-veen-yohn blahn
Moselle *(English spell.)*	mo-ZELL	Schloss	shlawss
Mourvèdre	moor-VED-ruh	sekt	zekt
Müller-Thurgau	MEW-lair TOOR-gao	Sémillon	seh-mee-yoh'n
Muscadet	mus-cah-day	Setúbal	SH TOO-bahl
Muscat	MUSS-cat	Seyval Blanc	say-vahl blahn
		Soave	SWAH-veh
Nahe	NAH-huh	Spätburgunder	SH PAYT-boor-guhn-der
Nebbiolo	neh-bee-OH-loh	spumante	spoo-MAHN-teh
Nierstein	NEER-sh'tine	Silvaner	sil-VAH-ner
		Syrah	see-rah
oenology	ee-NOLL-uh-jee		
oidium	oh-EE-dee-um	tannin	TAN-in
		Taurasi	tao-RAH-zee
Palomino	pahl-oh-MEE-noh	Tchelistcheff	Exactly the way it looks
Parducci	par-DOO-chee	Temecula	teh-MEH-kew-lah
Pauillac	paw-yak	Trentino-Alto	tren-TEE-noh AHL-toh
Pedro Ximénes	PAY-droh hee-MAY-nayss	Adige	AH-dee-jay
Pedroncelli	pehd-rawn-CHEL-ee	Tyrrell's	TIH-rehl's
Penedés	pay-nay-DAYSS		
Petite Sirah	peh-teet see-rah	Umpqua	UHMP-kwah
Phylloxera vastatrix	fill-OX-er-ah vahs-TAH-trix		
Piemonte	pee-yay-MON-teh	Valdepeñas	vahl-day-PAY-n'yahss
Piesport	PEEZ-port	Valpolicella	vahl-poh-leet-CHEL-ah
Pinot Grigio	PEE-noh GREED-jo	Veneto	VEN-eh-toh
Pinot Noir	pea-noh nwahr	Vichon	vee-shawn
Pouilly-Fumé	poo-yee foo-may	Vignoles	veen-yohl
Primitivo	pree-mee-TEE-voh	vin (s)	van (van)
Provence	pro-vahnss	vinho verde	VEEN-yoh VAIR-day
		Vitis vinifera	VIH-tiss vin-IF-er-ah
Quercus suber	KWAIR-cuss SOO-ber	Vouvray	voo-vray
Recioto	reht-CHOH-toh	Welbel	why-BELL
reservado	ray-ssair-VAH-tho	Willamette	wil AM ot
Retsina	ret-SEE-nah	Württemburg	ver-tem-bairg
Rheinpfalz	RINE-fahl'tz		
Rheingau	RINE-gao	Yakima	YAH-kuh-muh
Rheinhessen	rine-HESS-en		
Ribera del Duero	ree-BAY-rah dayl DWAY-roh	Zinfandel	zin-fan-dell

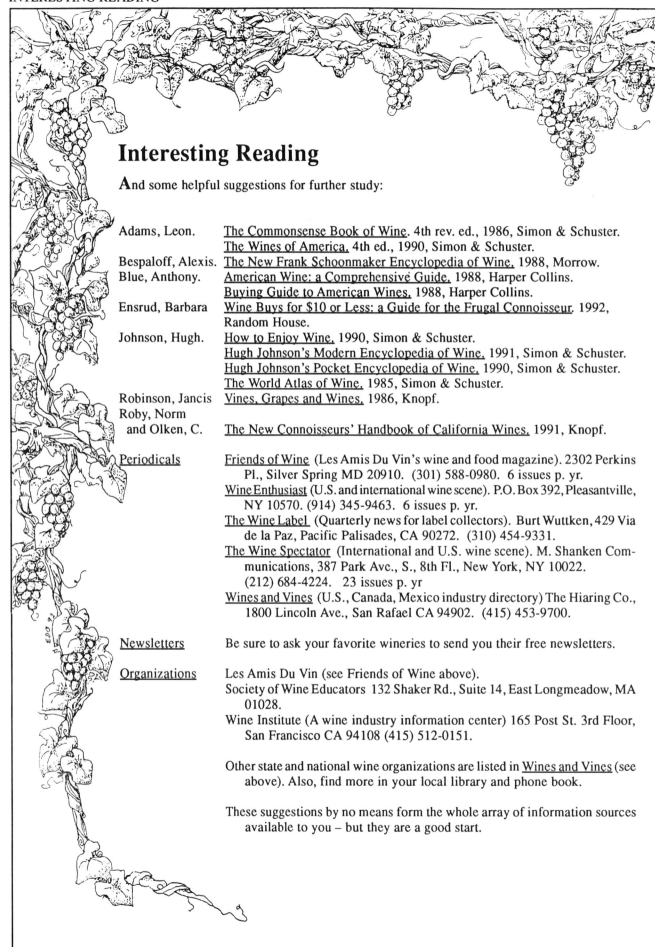

Interesting Reading

And some helpful suggestions for further study:

Adams, Leon.	The Commonsense Book of Wine. 4th rev. ed., 1986, Simon & Schuster.
	The Wines of America. 4th ed., 1990, Simon & Schuster.
Bespaloff, Alexis.	The New Frank Schoonmaker Encyclopedia of Wine. 1988, Morrow.
Blue, Anthony.	American Wine: a Comprehensive Guide. 1988, Harper Collins.
	Buying Guide to American Wines. 1988, Harper Collins.
Ensrud, Barbara	Wine Buys for $10 or Less: a Guide for the Frugal Connoisseur. 1992, Random House.
Johnson, Hugh.	How to Enjoy Wine. 1990, Simon & Schuster.
	Hugh Johnson's Modern Encyclopedia of Wine. 1991, Simon & Schuster.
	Hugh Johnson's Pocket Encyclopedia of Wine. 1990, Simon & Schuster.
	The World Atlas of Wine. 1985, Simon & Schuster.
Robinson, Jancis	Vines, Grapes and Wines. 1986, Knopf.
Roby, Norm and Olken, C.	The New Connoisseurs' Handbook of California Wines. 1991, Knopf.

Periodicals
   Friends of Wine (Les Amis Du Vin's wine and food magazine). 2302 Perkins Pl., Silver Spring MD 20910. (301) 588-0980. 6 issues p. yr.
   Wine Enthusiast (U.S. and international wine scene). P.O. Box 392, Pleasantville, NY 10570. (914) 345-9463. 6 issues p. yr.
   The Wine Label (Quarterly news for label collectors). Burt Wuttken, 429 Via de la Paz, Pacific Palisades, CA 90272. (310) 454-9331.
   The Wine Spectator (International and U.S. wine scene). M. Shanken Communications, 387 Park Avc., S., 8th Fl., New York, NY 10022. (212) 684-4224. 23 issues p. yr
   Wines and Vines (U.S., Canada, Mexico industry directory) The Hiaring Co., 1800 Lincoln Ave., San Rafael CA 94902. (415) 453-9700.

Newsletters
   Be sure to ask your favorite wineries to send you their free newsletters.

Organizations
   Les Amis Du Vin (see Friends of Wine above).
   Society of Wine Educators 132 Shaker Rd., Suite 14, East Longmeadow, MA 01028.
   Wine Institute (A wine industry information center) 165 Post St. 3rd Floor, San Francisco CA 94108 (415) 512-0151.

   Other state and national wine organizations are listed in Wines and Vines (see above). Also, find more in your local library and phone book.

   These suggestions by no means form the whole array of information sources available to you – but they are a good start.

Do you need another
Great Wine Adventure as a gift?

We'll bet that some of your friends would love to learn about wine –
surprise them with the wine games that teach.

Send our cover price (still the same, low....................$ 9.95
        plus California sales tax............................. .81
        plus shipping, tender care, and gift paper... 2.50
        ($2.50 for first book; $1.00 for ea. additional
              book to same address)   _____
                   TOTAL....$13.26

Include your address and
        your check or
    money order to: **Port Royal Publications**
                   16228 Estella Avenue
                   Cerritos CA 90701-1510
                   (310) 865-2888

*Your copy will be sent off within 5 working days of
receiving your order.*

Please ask for information about the beautiful
O.W.L.® **Official Wine Lover**® shirts and cups
and about Edie De Avila's new book, **Wine Challenge!**
It teases and torments experienced wine lovers with 50
new brainy, illustrated wine puzzlers.

Special thanks to...

Wendell Lee, State Counsel for the Wine Institute, Axel E. Borg, Wine Bibliographer, U. C. Davis, Scott Harvey of Santino Wines, Roger Cook of R & J Cook, Mark Jennings of Chateau Ste. Michelle, Bob Hartzell, President, California Association of Winegrape Growers, Fred Ransom of Rivendell Winery, Margaret Harding of Kendall-Jackson Vineyards, Dr. Richard Kepner, Chemistry Dept., U. C. Davis, and the librarians of the Cerritos, St. Helena, and Los Angeles public libraries.